The Capacity to Sin

Volume 3

Rayford Jones Elliott

This is a work of non-fiction. All scripture were taken from the King James Version of the Holy Bible, unless where otherwise noted.

CLF Publishing, LLC.
9161 Sierra Ave, Ste. 203C
Fontana, CA 92335
www.clfpublishing.org

Copyright © 2016 by Rayford Jones Elliott. All rights reserved. No portion of this book may be reproduced, stored in a retrieval system, or transmitted by any form or any means electronically, photocopied, recorded, or any other except for brief quotations in printed reviews, without the prior permission of the publisher.

Cover designed by Rayford J. Elliott

ISBN# 978-1-945102-09-7

Printed in the United States of America.

Dedication

This book is dedicated to you, simply because you have picked it up and it is in your hands. From my experience from *Capacity to Sin Volume I*, I found many people refused to touch the book simply because the word 'sin' tended to frighten them away. Sin is a big part of many people's lives, and they have become complacent with their lifestyle of sin. Therefore, because this book is in your hands, I take that to mean you have an interest in learning more about sin and perhaps you may even want to find ways to rid it from your life. You may have undesirable habits, things of a sinful nature, that are holding you back or perhaps you want to break away from some small habits in your life or you want to know more about how you can help someone else whom you know is bound with sin.

Again, to YOU I dedicate this book. I pray that you will find it to be very beneficial to you in your walk in life.

Acknowledgements

I want to thank my church, Love Peace and Happiness Family Christian Church, which I have been a member for fifteen years. During this period under the leadership of Bishop Leon Martin as pastor, I have grown tremendously in the Word of God and also in other aspects of my life.

Through Bishop's teaching of the Word and through the Living Word Bible College, sponsored by LPH Church, I have come to know God in a depth that I have never known. By taking part in ministries and being an active member, my relationship with God has become solidified. Thank you LPH Church, I will continue to work hard to be the servant of God you have taught me to be, as I continue to grow in His Word.

Lord, I give You the glory.

Preface

There are many obstacles in life that can keep the full benefits of God from us. This book has been written to address the biggest obstacle in our life that can impede us from receiving the blessings of God: sin.

This book is divided into twenty chapters that address sin. You will find that there are many repeats of certain kinds of sin throughout this book. This is because there are so many of the same sins repeated throughout the Bible.

This book is not designed to be read as just a story where it is important to start from the beginning. You can start in any chapter, and you will yet get the essence of the book's purpose. Moreover, this book fits in the category of a reference that addresses sin.

This is the third of three volumes. The first and second volumes address sin that was committed in the Old Testament Age and how to deal with each form of sin. This volume will address sins committed in the New Testament Age.

Table of Contents

Introduction		9
Chapter 1	Brother Sin Against Brother	13
Chapter 2	Take Away My Sin	17
	The Scroll	20
Chapter 3	Sin no More	21
Chapter 4	Without Sin	25
Chapter 5	Servant of sin	29
Chapter 6	Who Did Sin?	33
Chapter 7	Have No Sin	37
Chapter 8	Cloak for Sin	41
Chapter 9	Reprove the World of Sin	45
Chapter 10	The Greatest Sin	49
Chapter 11	Lay Not This Sin	51
	A Prayer	54
Chapter 12	All are Under Sin	55
Chapter 13	The Knowledge of Sin	59
Chapter 14	Impute Sin	63
Chapter 15	Death by Sin	67
Chapter 16	Law and Sin	41
Chapter 17	Sin Reigned unto Death	73
Chapter 18	Continue in Sin	75

Chapter 19	Death to Sin	79
Chapter 20	Free from Sin	83
Themes Verses		87
List of Common Sins and Their Causes		91
References		108
About the Author		109

Introduction

When man was created, sin did not yet exist in the earth realm. Man was made perfect in the image of God. But after the first man, Adam, and his wife, Eve, disobeyed God and ate from the forbidden tree of knowledge, sin came into existence for man. Man's first act of sin created the atmosphere: the capacity to sin by man. This capacity then trickled down to all subsequent generations of mankind.

Sin is the act that is used to destroy man's character, keeping him from his rightful place here on earth and from getting into heaven. Sin is any deed, action or words that go against God's instruction as inscribed in the Holy Bible. This act places man into a position to be condemned by God. It can destroy the very purpose for man's existence. Sin chokes and keeps out the spirit of God, which is the source of life and the force that drives man to eternity in heaven.

There are literally hundreds of ways to sin, but they all yield the same result – a ticket to Satan's kingdom. To truly understand sin, it is important that one understands its characteristics, its roots, its sources, its causes and effects as well as affects. Yes, sin has a character, which is reflected from its source: Satan.

Sin is predicated upon disobedience to God's Word. Many times, sin and disobedience are considered as separate acts or entities. However, one cannot exist without the other. If you disobey God's Word, you sin; if you sin, you are disobedient to His Word.

As you study the Bible, you will realize what sin is all about. It is a direct attack on the spirit of God within you. When a man does not know God, he is automatically participating in sin. Sin can also be a part of Christians' lives who are weak in their walk with God.

In warfare, you can strategically fight your battles by knowing your enemy and his dwelling place. The Bible tells us that Satan resides in the air (Ephesians 2:2). Therefore, as air is all around you,

Satan is in your presence at all times. This fact helps you to prepare for his attacks.

Satan's attacks have three objectives. One is temptation. Temptation is a tool Satan uses to get your attention. There are many tricks he uses to get you to yield to what he wants you to do; he uses deception, such as the lust of the flesh, lust of the eye, and the pride of life to lure you into his dominion.

To avoid these attacks, you should be made aware that God provides a way to avoid Satan's tactics and keep you from being consumed. He provides ways for you to remove yourself from diver temptations (Satan's attacks). One way God teaches us to fend off Satan's attack is stated in James 4:7: *"Submit yourselves therefore to God. Resist the devil, and he will flee from you."*

In this book, you will find Bible stories about how Satan used temptation to try and get people to submit to him. Some saints fell into his trap, while others did not. These stories will be addressed, and it will be explained how today you can apply God's strategy to resisting the devil in your life. After all, Satan is nothing but a paper tiger; you can easily defeat him with the Word of God.

The second objective of Satan's attack is actually falling into the act, thus committing sin. Satan rejoices at this point because he feels victorious. He may have won a battle at this point but not the war. This is why God sent our Lord and Savior Jesus Christ to redeem us from our sins. When you sin, it does not automatically put your name in the "book of hell's registration." Sin can be forgiven. You merely have to ask God for forgiveness. Thus, forgiveness can be seen as a tool that God has provided to directly defeat Satan's objectives.

The third objective is damnation in hell. At this stage, all three of Satan's objectives have been accomplished. Two opportunities in the first two objectives were missed: the opportunity to ward off temptation and to seek forgiveness for sin.

Hell is the final resting place for Satan's demons and their recruits. These are the ones who fell short of the glory of God. There will be no turning back. Thus, one will be condemned to hell and eternally burn in "fire and brimstone."

Because God allowed His son to come into this world, it is possible for you to be redeemed. His redemptive power allows you to be saved from the hand that is trying to snatch you away from eternal life in heaven and instead throw you into Satan's everlasting home.

If sin happens to come into your life, the scripture makes it clear that if you confess and repent, God will forgive your sins. Forgiveness is unconditional; there are no strings attached.

Satan may sometimes think that he has won a battle by sharpening his fiery dart, and he may become under the impression that he has won, but as believers we fight our battle offensively as well as defensively. Defensively, we as believers are constantly allowing the Word of God to penetrate our heart to ensure that sin is overcome in our life whenever it attacks. Offensively, the Word in our heart is propagated through our faith and through our mouth to rebuke the devil and all his demons' assaults.

In the Bible, "sin" is mentioned 389 times. When it is mentioned, most of the time, there is a story involved. This book will share some of the biblical accounts of sinful acts. Although there are literally hundreds of different types of sin, this book will cover a portion of these sins and their effects. However, you will find a list of over four hundred types and causes of sin in the back of the book.

I pray that the reading of this book will be a blessing and spiritually uplifting for you. God bless!

Capacity to Sin: Volume III

The Lord's Prayer

Our Father which art in heaven,

Hollowed be thy name.

Thy Kingdom come.

Thy will be done in earth,

as it is in heaven.

Give us this day our daily bread.

And forgive us our debts,

as we forgive our debtors.

And lead us not into temptations,

but deliver us form evil:

For thine is the kingdom, and the power,

and the glory, forever.

Amen

Chapter 1
Brother Sinning Against Brother

When one sins against another, he commits an act of wrongdoing to his brother that in some way creates harm or damage- physically, mentally or spiritually. It may appear when this act occurs that it only involve the ones who sin and the one whom was sinned against. However, in this situation, it is a trifold matter: This means that God is involved when one sins against another.

When a man sins, regardless of whether it is against another, or against himself, or against a group of people, or against family, etc...., all sins committed is against God. Because sin, wherever or to whomever it is directed toward, it is against the righteousness of God - If you sin against me, you sin against God.

Too often one sin against another person and it goes undetected even though it could have caused harm to the individual; this falls in the category of not loving one another which goes against the second great commandment Jesus gave to us. "Thou shalt love thy neighbor as thyself " (Mark 12:31).

There are many kinds of sin that one can commit against another. It all started from the sins Cain committed against his brother Able; this sinful act was an act of hate and pride but not love. As sin is committed against another, all fit into the same category, that is, to inflict harm on him; this what Cain action against his brother was all about.

Understanding that Jesus brought to us the power of forgiveness, whenever sin is against someone else, where should one seek forgiveness from, God or the brother? All sin, no matter where it is directed, one must first and always seek forgiveness from God. God is the one who can truly forgive sin: 1 John 1:9 states, *"If we confess our sins, he is faithful and just to forgive us our sins, and to cleanse us from all unrighteousness."*

God is always watching you from day to day. Nothing happens that He does not know. However, you may commit a sin against another and he may not have any knowledge of the act, but God knows.

Therefore, it is imperative that when one sin against a brother, forgiveness must first be sought from God. He is the one that has the power to forgive and open the door to a fulfilled life and to an everlasting life.

On the other hand, seeking forgiveness from your brother is important also because it can mend the relationship one has with the other and to alleviate or perhaps fix any damage that occurred as a result of the sinful act. However when you go to God first, He may give instructions on how to deal with the situation.

As the one who sins seeks forgiveness, likewise the one who was sinned against must forgive. This is what was addressed when the disciple approached Jesus questioning Him should a brother forgive one who sins against another. Matthew 18:21 says, *"Then came Peter to him, and said, Lord, how oft shall my brother sin against me, and I forgive him? till seven times?"* Matthew 18:22 says, *"Jesus saith unto him, I say not unto thee, Until seven times: but, until seventy times seven."* The disciple left the door open when he suggested forgiving seven times. By limiting the number of times to forgive someone implies one does not have to forgive when he doesn't feel it is necessary. Jesus told him seventy times seven, which implies you should always forgive.

Jesus used a parable to explain to the disciples why they should always forgive their brother that trespasses against them:

Matthew 18:23-35 (NIV) says, *"Therefore, the kingdom of heaven is like a king who wanted to settle accounts with his servants. As he began the settlement, a man who owed him ten thousand bags of gold was brought to him. Since he was not able to pay, the master ordered that he and his wife and his children and all that he had be sold to repay the debt.* "At this the servant fell on his knees before him. 'Be patient with me,' he begged, 'and I will pay back everything.' The servant's master took pity on him, canceled the debt and let him go. "But when that servant went out, he found one of his fellow servants who owed him a hundred silver coins. He grabbed him and began to choke him. 'Pay back what you owe me!' he demanded. "His fellow servant fell to his knees and begged him, 'Be patient with me, and I will pay it back.' "But he refused. Instead, he went off and had the man thrown into prison until he could pay the debt. When the other servants saw what had happened, they were outraged and went and told their master everything that had happened. "Then the master called the servant in. 'You wicked servant,' he said, 'I canceled all that debt of yours because you begged me to. Shouldn't you have had mercy on your fellow servant just as I had on you?' In anger his master handed him over to the jailers to be tortured, until he should pay back all he owed. "This is how my heavenly Father will treat each of you unless you forgive your brother or sister from your heart."*

As Christ stated, you should always forgive you brother. Even though there may or may not be a relationship between you, or even if this is someone whom you do not like, forgiveness of a brother's trespasses is always needed. It shows the love you have for your brother, and most of all, it shows the love and respect you have for God. This attitude and practice is appreciated and is pleasing to God.

It is important to note that if one commits a sin against another, God becomes the mediator. Consult Him if this happens, and He will give you guidance on how to handle the situation. Because God wants brothers to love one another.

Chapter 2
Take Away My Sin

One day when John the Baptist was baptizing in the Jordan River, he saw Jesus coming and immediately recognized him as the one who will make it possible for one's sin to be taken away. John 1:19 says, *"The next day John seeth Jesus coming unto him, and saith, Behold the Lamb of God, which taketh away the sin of the world."* Sinning can be perpetuated in all forms and manners, but Jesus came for the purpose of defeating the power of sin over anyone who comes to accept Him as the savior.

Historically, in the Old Testament, sin was dealt with by the priests, who accepted sacrifices from the people to atone for the sin they committed. Thus, there was a third party involved in dealing with one's sins: the priest. Priests did not have the power to forgive one's sin then, nor do they have the power today. Furthermore, the priests did not offer any guidance or way out to rid sin from one's life or how to live a righteous life even though people were faced with all types of adversities, as we do today. Sins were committed and addressed but there was no repentance. Believers paid the price they needed to pay to be "forgiven," but there was no emphasis on instilling in one's mind to turn away from the sin they committed to avoid committing the same sin again. Repentance was not emphasized.

As Jesus approached John, John realized it was the greatest day of all baptisms. Jesus was there to be baptized, and John would announce who he is. The greatest part of this occasion was that Jesus was not to be only baptized in the water by submerging, but He was to be baptized by the Holy Spirit. John 1:33 says, *"And I knew him not: but he that sent me to baptize with water, the same said unto me, up whom thou shalt see the Spirit descending, and remaining on him, the same is he which baptizeth with the Holy Ghost."* The baptism of the Holy Spirit came about by a dove that descended from heaven upon Jesus, which according to Matthew 3:16, was only visible to John and Jesus himself. This was a moment of divine empowerment in the ministry of Jesus. And of course, this was a confirmation to John the Baptist about who Jesus is.

This baptism, especially by the Holy Spirit, opened the door for all to turn away from sin by accepting Jesus as the savior. Once one accepts Him, it is up to the person to continue in Jesus' teachings in order to strengthen one's resolve against sin, the enemy of God's Word.

Jesus is the Lamb who forgives away your sin. However, He doesn't merely take away your sin, He makes the way for one to seek forgiveness through direct access to God's throne. Sin itself will always be in the atmosphere here on earth. It is not literally removed from man's presence or existence. Sin will remain here on earth until Satan himself is bound from access to God's people.

Sin is not taken away literally, it is merely forgiven, which means once God forgives a sin, it is not used against us the day we will all stand accountable for the wrong and good we have done. Our deeds, our faith, our righteousness and the type of life we lived are some of the criteria that defines our accountability during the days of judgment.

Once a sin is committed, it is done. There is no way to go back and correct it. As you are forgiven, it is up to you to stay on the right track and not commit the act anymore. As John the Baptist said, Jesus is the one who takes away our sin. What this statement translates into is what is given; salvation and the choice of not sinning anymore by living a righteous live.

Also, what it means by Jesus came and took away our sins is that He came and opened the kingdom of God to all and whosoever wants to live in His kingdom is welcome; the door is open. In His Kingdom, one is to live the life of righteousness. Righteousness is the way of life that allows one to live in His kingdom free from sinning. Righteousness can be seen as the opposite of sin. Sin is unrighteousness.

Before Jesus came, the blood of animals, such as lambs, was used to take away the sins of only the Jews. But when Jesus came, and shed His blood, His blood took away the sin of the whole world. That's what Jesus meant when He said in John 16:33, *"I have overcome the World."*

There are many blessings for those who allows Jesus, "the Lamb," to take away your sins. In order for this to happen, each person must come to and accept Him. This is the initial stage. Afterward, one must live his/her life according to the Word of God with dedication and commitment.

The Scroll

The Word of God was written on a scroll.
Read His word it will save you soul.
It was written, can't say exactly when.
It is proven, that it will defeat the attacks of sin.

The Word of God was written on a scroll.
What it will do only God knows.
It will fight your sin in day and night.
It will keep your battle in the line of sight.

The Word of God was written on a scroll.
In His Word He will keep you whole.
Read and learn His word with your heart.
There is nothing he will do for you because He's your God.

The Word of God was written on a scroll.
It Tells of Jesus, the greatest story ever told.
Jesus came to atone for out sin.
The world was full of sin, as it is now, not just then.

The Word of God was written on a scroll.
It tell us to go out and pass on its' message to all.
With the written word abiding in us we will not fall.
We will continue in the spirit to walk full and tall.

The Word of God was written on a scroll.
It will keep you out of Satan's pit.
When Satan fires his fiery dots, they will surely not stick.
With His Word you can be assure of Satan devices and tricks.
The Word of God was written on a Scroll.

Chapter 3
Sin No More

It is important to know that sin is an option, which means one does not have to sin. He can merely make a choice to commit the sin or not. This is what we all are faced with every day. As the scripture says, life and death result by the choices we make. Sin can be deadly.

It is wonderful to know that God is faithful to forgive our sin as stated in 1 John 1:9. When a sin is committed, God will forgive you and allow you a chance to repent. On the other hand, He truly expects you not to move back in the same old ways and do it again. John 5:14 states, *"Afterward Jesus findeth him in the temple, and said unto him, Behold, thou art made whole: sin no more, lest a worse thing come unto thee."*

This is what Jesus told the man He healed at the pool of Bethesda in Jerusalem. This man, for thirty-eight years, could not walk; he had spent his whole life lying in a bed because of this infirmity. This pool was a pool of water that could heal the first one who stepped in. At a certain season, an angel would come down and "trouble" (stir up) the water, and the first one who stepped into it would be healed. This man had been going to the pool for 38 years but did not have anyone to assist him in entering the pool; unfortunately, he missed out on his healing for thirty-eight years.

But, one day, Jesus came by the pool and when the man saw him, he asked Jesus for healing. Apparently, the man had heard about Jesus and the things He was doing to help people. Jesus, in the cripple man's presence, told him to pick up his bed and walk. The man followed Jesus' instruction and was healed.

Later, Jesus found the man in the temple and told him *"to sin no more"* (John 5:14). He also told him that *"lest a worse thing come unto thee."*

There are three profound lessons that are derived from the words of Jesus in this verse and the man's healing. First, it shows the sovereign power of Jesus, as it manifested in the power of healing. However, this was not the first healing or miracle Jesus had performed. But just the power of His words, *"pickup your bed up and walk,"* demonstrated His authoritative power.

The second lesson is *"to sin no more."* A question has come up many times: Can man live without sinning? There has always been division amongst believers due to this question; some say you can, and some say you can't. As mention many times before in all volumes of *The Capacity to Sin* books, sin is a choice. You choose to sin or not. It is up to you.

To choose not to sin anymore may be hard because of all of the challenges one goes through daily and the constant attacks of Satan through temptation. Satan has a kingdom, and this kingdom is a kingdom of sin and evil. He is moving like a lion roaring and trying to devour all he can to fill his kingdom through sin.

However, everyone can defeat Satan via the power God has given them through salvation and by merely take a stand and saying no to the devil's temptation. Taking this action will allow you to live a victorious life in God's kingdom. The first thing to be victorious in 'sinning no more' is developing strong faith, and above all, believe what Jesus says, what He did, and who He is.

Jesus told the healed man not to sin anymore. If Jesus told you not to do it then that implies that it can be done: that is sin no more. Jesus knows you can do it, and it is up to you to make the right choices to adhere to His words. Above all, you must believe you can do it. Scripture tell us in 1 John 3:9: *"Whosoever is born of God doth not commit sin; for his seed remaineth in him: and he cannot sin, because he is born of God."* Also Psalm 119:11 states, *"Thy word have I hid in mine heart, that I might not sin against thee."* It is simple enough, not to sin anymore - just hide His Word in your heart.

The third lesson of His words is *"lest a worse thing come unto thee."* Jesus knows you will be faced all kinds of temptations to lure you into diver temptation. Jesus is saying, whatever happens, whatever kind of attack you encounter, just say no to sin.

The question is can there be any victory in this battle? Yes, according to Corinthians, temptation you can bare whatever is trying to weigh you down to submit sin. 1 Corinthians 10:13 states, *"There hath no temptation taken you but such as is common to man: but God is faithful, who will not suffer you to be tempted above that ye are able; but will with the temptation also make a way to escape, that ye may be able to bear it."*

The three lessons in this scripture are summed up as follows: Jesus healed, Jesus advisee, and Jesus made provisions. Through these three lessons of Jesus, a born-again believer can most definitely avoid sinning. Jesus believes you can live without sinning, and He knows through His Word you can make the devil flee from you by living the life He has designed for you. So, just say no.

One must seriously believe and build a faith life that is unyielding in all aspects of life and allow Jesus' teaching to sit in the driving seat of his life. Faith, belief, and Jesus Christ are the tools to use to accomplish the "sin no more" life.

Some have said it is impossible to live without sinning anymore. But one cannot forget Philippians 4:13 which says, *"I can do all things through Christ which stengtheneth me."* With the strength of Christ, it is made possible. After all, Christ was tempted with three of the most inviting of all sins. He simply said no to Satan's temptation and deception.

One must always remember 1 Corinthians 10:13, which tells us that God provide us with the strength and encouragement to resist Satan's temptations, and God will open a door to escape his attacks. All we need to do is seek God for help, so we can be assured to choose the correct door: the door of righteousness.

Chapter 4
Without Sin

The Bible teaches us not to judge one another. However, there are situations where judgment is allowed, such as a games where you will find brothers competing against one another, or even in a court case where a designated person is authorized by law to make judgments about whether a person is guilty or not according to the secular law. The Bible teaches that it is not our job or duty to judge another because of the sin one has committed. When one commits sin, it is between him and God, whether judgment will take place or not. God is the one who will have the final say so about sin. However, it is up to the person to seek forgiveness from God for this dreadful act and to eradicate the sin in his life.

Oftentimes, there is one who would accuse another of sin, and he himself is guilty of the same sin. People accuse and persecute others in so many ways to either bring harm to or to gain attention in the action against a person who has sinned. The old saying about the sweeping is so true: "sweep around your own front door before you start sweeping around mine."

It is noteworthy to understand what happened when Jesus, early one morning, came from Mount Olive and entered into the temple again. There were scribes and Pharisees who brought an accused woman into the temple court, and they accused her of committing adultery. They introduced her to Jesus as a woman who had sinned by committing adultery and wanted to know what Jesus thought should be done. The scribes and Pharisees said she should be stoned because of her sin: This type of punishment for sin was a part of the Old Testament law. However, their real reason for bringing the woman to the temple was they were really not concerned about carrying out the law. They wanted to test Jesus. They were trying to discredit Him for who He is. They expected Jesus to go against the law and pardon her of her sin; then, they could arm themselves with ammunition to feed their desire to discredit Him.

There was a crowd of people in the court of the temple, and they were all there looking and wondering what Jesus' response would be toward what the scribes and Pharisees were asking of Him. Jesus' response was in John 8:7 states, *"He that is without sin among you, let him first cast a stone at her."*

Jesus did not answer them immediately. He continued what he was doing at the moment, and they continued asking him, until he finally lifted himself and responded. Apparently, they did not understand that Christ came not to condemn man, but to bring sinners to repentance and salvation. As Romans 8:1 states, *"There is therefore now no condemnation to them which are in Christ Jesus, who walk not after the flesh, but after the Spirit."*

Jesus responded to the situation with a question (John 8:7), which immediately caused all the accusers to leave the scene expeditiously. That included the Pharisees and scribes.

The woman remained at the scene with Jesus. Jesus looked up at her, and there was no one in the court but her and few onlookers. He told her He would not condemn her. Instead, He sent her on her way with instructions, telling her not to sin anymore. John 8:11explains, *"She said, No man, Lord, and Jesus said unto her, Neither do I condemn thee: go and sin no more."*

The accusers left but there remained in the court other Pharisees and onlookers. Jesus spoke to them and told them He is the light of the world and any man that follows him will not walk in darkness (John 8:12).

What Jesus was telling them was that all have sinned but our sin can be forgiven if we walk with Him. Sin is the dark side of life and this darkness can be blotted out by Him, the light that He shines.

Jesus, through this incident, showed what the world was like then and now. He showed what He is all about and why He came to this world. As they all fled, that showed that they were all guilty of sin in their life. During that time and today, all are guilty of it, and no man lives without some kind of committed sin. Romans 3:23 states, *"For all have sinned, and come short of the glory of God."*

He did not accuse the accusers nor did he accuse the woman. This was because he came to save the world and not to destroy it. He would have loved it if everyone that was there would have come to repentance. He wanted them to seek forgiveness for their sin. However, they refused to do so by fleeing the scene.

This was a good opportunity for all the sinners there to come to repentance. But, they chose to run. As for the woman whose sin was exposed by the accusers, He showed mercy and forgiveness by sending her on her way and not punishing her for what she had done. The Pharisees and Scribes accusers wanted to see Jesus go against the law, but they did not stay around long enough to see/hear His decision.

But, it must be noted that she did not leave without instruction from Jesus. Today, these instructions are applicable to all today as we walk this life. The woman was guilty of sin as well as the accusers. As a matter of fact, the accusers were sinning that very moment because they were being judgment on what she had done.

Before anyone starts making accusations about one's sinful life, he should always look in the mirror. Look at yourself and ask God to examine you and blot out all iniquity and sin in your life. Psalm 26:2 states, *"Examine me, O Lord, and prove me; try my reins and my heart."* Seek guidance from God. If you see one in sin, pray for him, pray for deliverance.

The accusers' objective was to trap Jesus. They distorted their own law to entrap Him. They brought only the woman as the sinner in this situation. But what happened to the other party involved in her adulterous act? The sin was adultery, and it takes two to commit this act. They left the man out. According to their law, in Leviticus 20:10 says, *"And the man that committeth adultery with another man's wife, even he that committeth adultery with his neighbour's wife, the adulterer and the adulteress shall surely be put to death."*

The accusers were distorting their own law, yet implying that they were without sin. But, they were sinners not in upholding the law, but in other areas. Jesus said He is the light of the world. They were walking in the light of the law and did not have a spirit-filled life. Therefore, they were walking in darkness.

They knew not Jesus. They did not know how to ask forgiveness when sin happens in their life. No one is without sin, but the key is for you to seek forgiveness and repent. Repent and turn away from the sin. Therefore, you will not walk in darkness but walk in the light, the light of Jesus. Seek the light Jesus is shining in your life daily.

Chapter 5

Servant of Sin

In John 8:34, Jesus said one can become a servant to sin. To be a servant is to render service to someone else and to placate him or please him with what you do for him by exorcising his wishes or desired. One adheres and supports the wishes of someone else or the one who has him bound to his wishes. In essence, a servant always does what someone else wants, to please him in many aspects. One can be a servant by providing a service economically, politically, socially, physically, psychologically, and spiritually.

To be a servant is to represent the thoughts, ideas and beliefs of one has toward another. Although one can serve as a servant for his own personal gain, the focal point of this chapter is on one serving others. Either way a servant renders service to placate someone else regardless of the reason why he is a servant.

As a servant, it is important to look at who really benefits from serving. There could be either benefit for the served or the server. The servant can serve to please himself as in the case of someone serving for a reward, to pay a debt, or it could be mere pleasure. There could be someone serving just to please someone else out of dedication, responsibility, or requirement.

A servant can also be looked upon as a slave; that is, if someone is either forced to serve someone without his consent; he may find himself in a difficult situation where he will find it hard to release himself from the forced services.

On the other hand, a slave to something could be characterized by one habits or selfish desires. To say that someone is a slave to something could also mean that a person is strongly influenced or controlled by something or someone.

Jesus addressed the fact that some are or could be slaves, as servant to sin. John 8:34 states, *"Jesus answered them, Varily, Varily, I say unto you, Whosoever committeth sin is the servant of sin."* Most Bible translations use the phrase "slave" instead of "servant." For example, the NLV translation states, *"...I tell you the truth, everyone who sins is a slave of sin."* The NIV translation is *"...Very truly I tell you, everyone who sins is a slave to sin."* They all have the same meaning and are addressing the repercussions for sinning.

There was a gathering of Jewish believers whom Jesus was speaking to. He told them if they really knew the truth then the truth would set them free. They misunderstood what Jesus was speaking about. They, however, were believers, but they believed in what Jesus could do but not who He is.

Their response was that they were children of Abraham and they have never been slave to anyone. However, Jesus was not speaking of a physical slavery but a spiritual one which was bound by Satan's weapon of mass destruction, sin.

To be a slave to sin means you are bound by its spiritual shackles. These shackles are fleshly based and are categorized by the lust of the flesh, the lust of the eye, and the pride of life. They are habitual, and the one who is caught up in this bondage situation find it very difficult to break away from it. The shackle of sin cannot be broke by itself. It takes knowledge, understanding, love, and standing strong in one's determination and the power of God.

Knowledge and understanding are manifested by knowing the Father, the Son, and the Holy Spirit. In other words, knowing who Jesus Christ is in conjunction with what He has done for all mankind. His love for you will set you free from sin. Jesus made the statement: *"Now the slave does not remain in a household forever; the son [of the master] does remain forever"* (John 8:35 AMP).

A servant can also be looked upon as a slave; that is, if someone is serving and finds himself in a difficult situation in terms of releasing the services being rendered; there is no liberty; it is a slave rendering service but doing so under unwilling conditions.

A slave to sin is someone who has allowed the flesh nature to overcome the spiritual natural. The flesh nature is built on sinful activities. These activities are done to satisfy the flesh, which manifests itself as satisfying one selfish desires in the things to which they render service.

To reiterate the relationship of a servant to sin, one can easily become a slave to sin. Because sin pleases Satan, it is a service rendered to him. A slave to sin is a servant to Satan. As Jesus states in John 8:34, *"Jesus answered them, Verily, verily, I say unto you, Whosoever committeth sin is the servant of sin."*

There were Jewish believers who believed Him, but yet they would question Him. But, Jesus was responding to the Jew who did not understand what is referenced here as slave. They told Jesus they were seeds of Abraham, and they never have been in bondage. They apparently had forgotten what happened to their people in Egypt and other captivities that occurred throughout their history. But, Jesus was not speaking of a physical slave but as a spiritual slave or bondage.

This type of situation is prevalent today in so many people's lives. But what is so tragic about it is that most people are in spiritual bondage and are not aware of it. They live their lives being satisfied with where they are and what they are doing. They do not realize there is liberty through Jesus and their lives can be so much better in all areas. They are missing out on all of the blessings God has in stored for them.

There are ways to break away from being a servant of sin or a slave to sin. This way is through Jesus Christ. He has already set you free and all you have to do is take off the shackles of sin; Jesus is the Key. Use Him.

2 Corinthians 3:17 (ESV) *"Now the Lord is the Spirit, and where the Spirit of the Lord is, there is freedom."*

John 8:32 (ESV) *"And you will know the truth, and the truth will set you free."*

Galatians 5:1 (ESV) *"For freedom Christ has set us free; stand firm therefore, and do not submit again to a yoke of slavery."*

Chapter 6

Who Did Sin?

One of the most profound teachings of Jesus Christ is on making judgments of others. This is something that is very common today in this world. It can be found time and again that someone is making a judgment on another. It happens in the secular world, as well as in the spiritual world. In the spiritual world, we have Christians and true believers making accusations about sin. Whether it is true or not, sin is not to be judged or justified by man: This is God's area of work.

There is a story in the Bible that shows how others can easily make judgments. Jesus was with His disciples when they came to a blind man who had been blind since his birth. They asked Jesus who had sinned, the blind man or his parents. They were attributing his blindness as a result of a sin that he or his parents had committed. Their mentality was that all sickness or illness is a result of sin.

Another example was people relating sin to mishaps in life of the eighteen Galileans (Luke 13:4), who died as a result of the collapse of the tower of Siloam. Some of the disciples and others felt that the death of the eighteen was caused by the sin they had committed. They thus concluded that sinners will die of this kind of tragedy.

They thought that their sin (the eighteen killed at Siloam) was above all others in the city and that's why they were killed in this tragedy. Jesus addressed this question by pointing out that the cause of a person's death is not necessarily an indication on how they lived. Luke 13: 4-5 says, *"Or those eighteen, upon whom the tower in Siloam fell, and slew them, think ye that they were sinners above all men that dwelt in Jerusalem? I tell you, Nay: but, except ye repent, ye shall all likewise perish."*

Some people today want to know what sin someone has done to cause their sickness; but, God's sovereign power cannot be neglected. The sovereign power of God allowed sickness to come upon Job, but not due to a sin he committed.

The disciples with Jesus were making accusations or making judgments on the blind man or his parents. By them asking that question made it clear that in their eyes sin causes illness or sickness. The verse in discussion here is John 9:2, which states, *"And his disciples asked him, saying, Master, who did sin, this man, or his parents, that he was born blind?"* Note that the man was born blind; therefore, he could not have committed a sin. He, however, was born into a sinful world or environment. An unborn child cannot commit a sin.

When Jesus and His disciples came upon the blind man, Jesus spat on the ground, made mud, took it, and put it over the man's eyes. He then told the blind man to go *"wash in the Pool of Siloam"* (John 9:7 Quest Study Bible). The man went, and after he was done washing the mud from is eyes, everything became visible to him. He could see.

The blindness and the healing must be seen as God's divine purpose and His sovereign power. The question should not be asked who sinned, in an effort to place blame or judgment. Surely, one may see one sinning, as a believer in God, you would know sin when you see it or hear it; thus, we are to pray and help them.

The environment we all live in today, sin is surely an everyday occurrence. But, even if one of life's mishaps happens to someone, it should not be said it happened because of a sin. Problems and mishaps happen to sinners, "non-sinner", believers and non-believers.

Surely as misfortunes or tragedies happen in life, which is something all will experience somewhere along their life's stay here on earth, that is not the time to raise questions about what they did or who did it. It is a time to take in and use God's guidelines (His Word) about how we can learn from it. Use it as a time to thank God for his unchangeable hand that is stretched out to pull us through. God's hand through Jesus Christ reached out and healed the blind man. The people of the tower of Siloam died, but it was not the time for judging and blaming. Jesus' response to their question was that knowing that all have sinned and come short of the glory of God, the focus should be on repenting.

The Beatitudes

Blessed are the poor in spirit:
for theirs is the kingdom of heaven.
Blessed are they that morn:
for they shall be comforted.
Blessed are the meek:
for they shall inherit the earth
Blessed are they which do hunger and thirst after righteousness:
for they shall be filled.
Blessed are the merciful:
for they shall obtain mercy.
Blessed are the pure in heart:
for they shall see God.
Blessed are the peacemakers:
for they shall be called the children of God.
Blessed are they which are persecuted
for righteousness sake:
for theirs is the kingdom of heaven.
Blessed are ye, when men shall revile you, and persecute you, and
shall say all manner of evil against you falsely, for my sake.

Chapter 7
Have No Sin

Anytime someone sins, God requires that he seeks forgiveness and come to repentance. This is something that all believers know. The Bible teaches all about sin and the coming, leaving, and returning of Jesus Christ. It tells us He came into this world not to condemn it, but to save it. John 3:16-17 so explicitly explains, *"For God so loved the world, that he gave his only begotten Son, that whosoever believeth in him should not perish, but have everlasting life. For God sent not his Son into the world to condemn the world; but that the world through him might be saved."*

What is said in the above two verses is that Jesus Christ was sent by His Father to save the world from its sin because sin is destructive, and it is the way of Satan. Satan's purpose is to kill, steal, and destroy man, by keeping him from eternal life, but Jesus Christ came to give us life, a more abundant life by saving us from the devil's evil tactics. Jesus came and made it possible to destroy all of Satan's vices: Satan's vices' effects are stated in 1 John 3:8

"He that committeth sin is of the devil; for the devil sinneth from the beginning. For this purpose, the Son of God was manifested, that he might destroy the works of the devil." Thus, God sent His son to save mankind from sin.

Sin has been in existence on earth from the beginning of man. Satan infiltrated man's environment and caused him to sin, thus creating a sinful nature for man. This sinful nature has become a way of life for man throughout history. However, Jesus Christ made it possible to be saved from it. Although the sinful environment or nature of man has caused every man to some degree to have committed sin. In this environment, man has been given the tools to defeat the enemy (sin) if used properly.

It is important to know the repercussions of committing sin. Romans 6:23 states, *"For the wages of sin is death; but the gift of God is eternal life through Jesus Christ our Lord."*

Now that we know that sin can lead to death, scripture tells us that all have sinned. Romans 3:23 states, *"As it is written, there is none righteous, no, not one:"* This scripture also tells us: *"For all have sinned, and come short of the glory of God."*

With this being said, it is clear that sin is present throughout the world, and it is necessary for everyone to recognize when it becomes a part of one's life. If someone does not recognize this, then he is spiritually blinded. John 9:41 states, *"Jesus said unto them, If ye were blind, ye should have no sin: but now ye say, We see; therefore your sin remaineth.* Thus *"For all have sinned, and come short of the glory of God"* (Romans 3:23). Understanding this will make one aware and open to the fact that no one is immune from sin in his life.

There are so many instances when one is blinded to sin. As such, he is blinded and in essence, denying that sin is in his life. If the sin is not recognized and one does not have guilt of such an act or acts (sin), he is forfeiting his right for forgiveness. Forgiveness is the tool to pardon you from your sin.

If one says he has not sinned or is aware of it and continues to deny it, then he is strengthening his spiritual blindness. To say or think in such a way, one will perpetuate his sinful life or *"therefore your sin remaineth."* 1 John 1:8 states, *"If we say that we have no sin, we deceive ourselves, and the truth is not in us."*

Capacity to Sin: Volume III

Chapter 8

Cloak for Sin

One of the characteristics of a sinner is the attempt to hide his sin. Hiding sin is not new. It has been practiced by people for centuries. As a matter of fact, it was attempted to be hidden from the beginning of mankind. Namely Adam, he sinned and tried to cover his sin with fig leaves. He tried to override God's law by making excuses. Evidently, he was not aware of the ole saying that "excuses only serve those who make them." Adam's mistake was he did not know God is always watching.

No matter what the sin is, it cannot be justified, excused, or taken back. Once a sin is committed, it is done. However, there are attempts in using something that can be used to justify or excuse sin, but this is only done in an effort to satisfy man. In this case, it is dealing with the flesh. But with God, it is unacceptable and will not work in the spiritual realm of life. There is no justifying sin.

If God had not spoken to Adam, he would have continued to live his life thinking that by hiding himself with a fig leaf would eradicate his sin. One can cloak sin or try to prevent his sin from being seen, excuse sin, or even justify sin. But, God is the one and only one who knows all of your sins. He sees all things and knows all things. There is nothing hidden from God. He is the Great "I AM." All power is in His hand.

John 15:22 says, *"If I had not come and spoken unto them, they had not had sin: but now they have no cloak for their sin."* If man is of the world, then his action or sin is of the world. The world will judge man's own actions, which makes it so easy to vindicate, alleviate, justify, and cloak sin with their tactics, which will be to no avail. The world cannot offer what God has to offer, namely everlasting life, forgiveness and will not hold what you have done against you.

To cloak a sin does not keep the sin away from God's eyes. It only perpetuates the whole action because it is not meeting the requirement God has set in place to deal with sin.

There are other characters in the Bible that tried to cloak their sins. King Saul is a good example of someone trying to using a cloak. When Saul went to battle, he was told by the prophet to destroy all of the spoils of the enemy after the victory in the battle against the Philistines. He won the victory but did not follow the instructions or commands that were given to him from God by the prophet. Instead of destroying the spoils of the enemy, he took it upon himself to hoard the spoil. When he was approached by the prophet who represented God, Saul used lies to try and cover up his disobedience to the instructions that were given to him.

As soon as he begins to speak lies, the prophet knew immediately that he had not done what God had told him to do or carry out the commands from God. But little did he know, God was watching, seeing all that took place. Numbers 32:23 states, *"But if you would not do so, behold, you have sinned against the Lord, be sure your sin will find you out."*

The prophet pointed out Saul's sin. If he had not pointed it out, Saul would've continued trying to cloak, hide, and cover his sin.

One must understand that even though someone may not accost you and bring forth your sin to light, God already knows about it. As a matter of fact, He is the one who will judge it.

This is why it is so important for everyone to soak themselves in the Word of God. By doing so, you fortify, build your relationship with God and His Word. In this strong relationship you build with God, there will be no room for hiding sin. God will give you a discernment for sin and make you fully aware that sin must be forgiven.

Capacity to Sin: Volume III

Chapter 9
Reprove the World of Sin

It is important to understand and know the role the Holy Spirit plays in sin. Jesus came and set the stage for sin problems that impede man's ability to live a righteousness life and to know what to do when one is confronted with temptation (Satan's weapon). Sin is the tool that Satan uses to recruit God's children into his (Satan) kingdom.

Jesus came to save man from falling into Satan's trap of sin. He brought to the forefront the work of sin and convinced the world that sin is the tool of the enemy and the affect it has on one's life.

Christ was physically on earth for a short period of time- 33 years to be exact. He knew that His time was short and He had to make a way to help man when confronted by sin. He taught, trained, and led men (His disciples) to prepare for His leaving. He knew because of His love for us, that He could not leave man without leaving in the midst of man a form of a helpmate to help man during his trials, struggles, and persecutions because the enemy is strong in his tactics.

Man can be strong, but it would require time, spiritual growth, and spiritual development before man is able to stand before the enemy face to face with the conviction to say no to the enemy. Because man is a being that has a flesh body that is vulnerable to attack, that's what the enemy goes after, or tries to get man to submit to him.

Who was this helpmate Jesus left for support of man as he walks through life? He is the Holy Spirit. The Holy Spirit is a spirit being who is available for everyone who believes in the incarnate Christ and allows and accepts Him to help and provide the guidance and support to be victorious over man's sinful nature.

John 16:7-8 tell us in Jesus' own words that He will send the Holy Spirit. But in order for that to take place, Jesus' plan was that He will have to leave this world. *"Nevertheless I tell you the truth; It is expedient for you that I go away: for if I go not away, the comforter will not come unto you. And when he is come, he will reprove the world of sin and of righteousness, and of judgement: of sin, because they believer not on me; of righteousness, because I go to my Father, and ye see me no more; of judgement, because the prince of this world is judged"* (John 16:7-11). Note- Jesus called the Holy Spirit a "comforter." Comforter and Holy Spirit are synonymous.

The question that may arise is how does the Holy Spirit work or help man? He (the Holy Spirit) dwells inside of believers that receive Him. His work is explained in John 16:8; *"and when he come he will convict the world concerning sin and righteousness, and judgement"* (ESV). What Christ meant is that the world is a sinful place, and He (the Holy Spirit) will convince man in this world that sin is real and active. Therefore, man would not be ignorant of its existence and devices. 2 Corinthians 2:11 says, *"Lest Satan should get an advantage of us: for we are not ignorant of his devices."*

The Holy Spirit also shows man righteousness. Righteousness is acting according to the divine commands and law that are set forth to believer to adhere to. The Holy Spirit that dwells in you will guide you to continue to walk on the right side of the fence and encourage you to say no to the Satan.

As for judgment is concerned, the Holy Spirit will show how Christ's spirit is greater than Satan's. One can choose to walk with Christ or Satan. Walking with Christ will result in great benefits and blessings. Walking with Satan is damnation.

Jesus said that He (the Comforter) will in essence expose the world of it sin and its master Satan. He said that He will reprove the world of sin. Reprove is to correct in a gentle way, according to Webster Dictionary. The Holy Spirit will assist and provide the correct choice when you are faced with the temptations of sin as it tries to get you to yield to it.

It can be seen then that man is not alone when confronted with sins, whether it is fornication, lying, adultery, hating your brother, covertness, stealing, malice, unforgiving, etc.… Believers are not on the battle field by themselves. You are not on in this battle as one, but two. The first one is you and the other one is the Holy Spirit, who is the commander who prescribes the correct order. And it is up to you to be disciplined enough to carry out what the Holy Spirit is telling you.

By being obedient to His commands, He will help you to obtain the fruit of the spirit that are prescribed in the book of Galatians. Galatians 5:22-23 says, *"But the fruit of the Spirit is love, joy, peace, longsuffering, gentleness, goodness, faith, meekness, temperance,"* and with these fruit, which will become manifested in your character, you will find it easy to say no to sin.

These fruit will also help build a fence around you with the Word of God. Thus, it will be hard, very difficult, or impossible for sin to penetrate your life. You will become stronger. These characteristics, along with the Holy Spirit, will help you to continue to uphold the righteousness of God over sin.

Proverbs 29:15 shows the advantage of the Comforter being a part of your life. *"The rod and reproof give wisdom: but a child left to himself bringeth his mother to shame."* This points out again that we do not have to be alone when confronted with sin. It is not wise when confronted to make a decision or choose a direction without conscious consultation with Him.

Hebrews 12:5-11 from the NIV version clearly explains the important of reproof. *"And have you completely forgotten this word of encouragement that addresses you as a father addresses his son? It says, "My son, do not make light of the Lord's discipline, and do not lose heart when he rebukes you, because the Lord disciplines the one he loves, and he chastens everyone he accepts as his son." Endure hardship as discipline; God is treating you as his children. For what children are not disciplined by their father? If you are not disciplined—and everyone undergoes discipline—then you are not legitimate, not true sons and daughters at all. Moreover, we have all had human fathers who disciplined us and we respected them for it. How much more should we submit to the Father of spirits and live! They disciplined us for a little while as they thought best; but God disciplines us for our good, in order that we may share in his holiness. No discipline seems pleasant at the time, but painful. Later on, however, it produces a harvest of righteousness and peace for those who have been trained by it."*

The Holy Spirit will help you by making sure you have knowledge, understanding, and wisdom to deal with a sinful situation. It therefore is imperative that every believer understand who and where He is. One must be aware of His spiritual being that dwells inside of you, and let your heart and mind listen to Him when He speaks to you. He will surely guide you away from a sinful lifestyle to the path of righteousness.

Chapter 10

The Greater Sin

One sin that is considered to be a great sin is the sin of wrongful judgment resulting in the betrayal and crucifixion of one. That's what happened to Jesus. Jesus' death came about by betrayal and jealousy. What makes it even worse is that it was His people who were responsible for His death.

After Jesus was arrested by the Jewish authorities, they wanted to permanently remove Him from society because to them they felt He was a threat to their authority. They wanted Him killed because they refused to accept Him for who He is; they would not accept who He is in any way. Therefore, the only way via their sinful ways they could deal with Him was to have him crucified.

However, they did not want to crucify Him themselves because they wanted to keep their hands clean with the many followers of Jesus. They knew that killing him themselves would make it look bad or perhaps cause an uprising within the Jewish community.

When Jesus was taken by Pilate, he questioned Jesus, had him flogged, had his men make a wire crown and put on his head and threw a purple rob around him. He then took Him outside of his quarters and presented him to the Jewish crowd as they awaited him.

Pilate told them he found no fault in Him. And immediately, the high priest in the Jewish crowd yelled out saying, "Crucify him!" because He said He is the son of God.

When Pilate heard this, he became afraid and took Jesus back into his compound and questioned Jesus again. He asked Jesus, *"Where are you from?"* But, Jesus gave him no answer. So, Pilate said to him, *"You will not speak to me? Do you not know that I have authority to release you and authority to crucify you?"* (ESV). And Jesus responded with the following statement. John 19:11 says, *"You would have no authority over me at all unless it had been given you from above. Therefore, he who delivered me over to you has the greater sin."*

Pilate, of course, had the authority to free him or crucify him. As such, Pilate "was guilty of cowardice and the unjust use of his authority. But there was one, Caiaphas (the priest), was guilty of a greater sin because he knew about Jesus' miracles and ministry, yet his hatred and envy cause him to condemn Jesus (John 11:49-50, Quest Study Bible).

The sin of Jesus' Jewish counterpart was greater than Pilate's misuse of his power. To betray the son of God is equivalent to blasphemy.

The Jewish leaders had no authority to crucify anybody; this was a method the Roman government used to deal with criminals. And of course, Jesus is no criminal. The priest and the rest of the Jewish leaders that were there wanted Jesus out of the way because they felt threatened by the power of Jesus' leadership and ministry.

Chapter 11
Lay Not This Sin

It is wonderful to know Jesus and who He is, to know His character and what He is. Two of His biggest characteristics are humility and love. Humility because He always shows the concern He has for others and put others first then and now. He humbled Himself when He was attacked by His enemy, when one did wrong against Him, and when He was persecuted.

Ordinarily, these qualities can be difficult for believers or Christians today. They somehow find the challenges they are facing too hard or too difficult to manifest these qualities. Thus, it is important to develop these qualify, so they will be a part of your everyday life, not just when challenges occur.

In the midst of any struggle in life, one should always continue to glorify God. Glorifying God is manifested through one's humility and love for God. Having these qualities is so important because if one doesn't, he will focus on himself instead of God, who brings to us victory and wisdom in life.

We should always understand and be aware that the spirit of God is upon us, as God was in Jeremiah 29:11, *"I know the thoughts I have toward you, thoughts of good and not evil and that you should have an expected end."* Thus, for example, if one does you wrong, and you should have a willing heart of forgiveness.

The character of love which Jesus possesses is so powerful until nothing can compare. The scripture reveals to us the essence of why Jesus came to this earth. John 3:16-17 says, *"For God so loved the world, that he gave his only begotten Son, that whosoever believeth in him should not perish, but have everlasting life. For God sent not his Son into the world to condemn the world; but that the world through him might be saved."*

Even when Jesus was crucified, He showed His love for us as well as His enemies, or the ones who had persecuted and crucified Him on the cross. With His enemies standing in His presence as He was about to take the natural death, His Word was to *"forgive them for they did not know what was doing."*

Ordinarily, once in this type of situation, anyone else would have responded with a much negative response, such as wishing harm upon their persecutors or enemies. However, it is a sin to wish harm upon another, regardless of the circumstances.

There was another man that was so powerfully strong in his belief in Christ that he had the same spiritual characteristics as Christ. This man was no other than the martyrdom Stephen. Stephen was an evangelist and deacon. He preached the kingdom of God and Christ. For this, he was persecuted and stoned to death because of his love for Christ and his fellow brothers (brothers, whether friend, or foe).

Stephen gave a speech in the temple in the presence of God. His speech started with a history of the patriarch and their relationship with God. Abraham, as he begun, was in Mesopotamia, where he was in God's presence and God appeared to him and told him, *"Get the out of thy country, and from thy kindred, and come into the land which I shall shew thee"* (Acts 6:3). Stephen made the point that God's presence is not just in the temple, but God is everywhere. God is omnipresent. At that point, the Pharisees and Sadducees accused him of blasphemy and took him to the Sanhedrin court and had him stoned to death. The ones who was responsible for paving the way for Stephen to be persecuted and the ones who stoned him to death became his enemies.

However, because of Stephen's humble heart, love for his brothers, and his great love for Christ and the kingdom of God, he asked for forgiveness for them in his dying moment. The scripture tells us in Act 7:60 says, *"And he kneeled down, and cried with a loud voice, Lord, lay not this sin to their charge. And when he had said this, he fell asleep."* What this verse means is that Stephen was asking for forgiveness for his enemies. He did not want this sin of persecution and murdering of him held against his foes. He was so full of love and strong in the Word of God that he chose to offer himself as a living sacrifice for the Word of God and His kingdom.

Stephen could have very well saved himself, perhaps by retracting what he stood for or sought leniency for his life. But the Word was so strong in him, so that obedience and his love for the Word of God for him were better than sacrifice. As Stephen did – you must stand strong in the name of Jesus amongst all your adversities.

When someone sins against you, don't seek revenge or let hatred enter your heart. You must pray about it and allow the Holy Spirit to lead you in the right direction and help you humble yourself.

A Prayer

Take us to the king. Lord, take us and use us. We give ourselves to you oh, mighty God, who has saved us from our iniquity and our sins. We stretch our hand to you today. Take our hand, oh, Lord and lead us. Lead us up the path of righteousness, oh God. Take our hand, oh God. Lead us to victory in our life, oh God. Take our hand, lead us to the path of knowledge, lead us to the path of love, lead us to the path of meekness, lead us to the path of humbleness, lead us to the path of healing, lead us to the path of peace, lead us to the path of forgiving, lead us oh, Lord, as we give ourselves away to you. Oh Lord, keep the light shining in our pathway; keep the lamp unto our feet. Oh Lord, forgive us of all of our sin, oh Lord!

Chapter 12

All Are Under Sin

It is well known that there is not one who is not guilty of sin. If you believe in the Word of God, it tells us this. Romans 3:10 says, *"As it is written, There is none righteous, no, not one."* Romans 3:23 says, *"For all have sinned, and come short of the glory of God."* In some way or form, there is a sin that all have committed sometime in their life.

We were born into a sinful environment. The very day that we came out of our mother womb, we were cast into this environment. As a baby, you don't know right from wrong, good or evil, or love or hate. Knowing the difference is a process of development and growth: spiritually, physically, ethically, morally, psychologically, and in the Word of God. But even as one grows up in these areas just mentioned, the sinful environment becomes an enticing environment.

This enticing environment is something that Satan makes available. Because it is his objective is to seek and devour all he can to come over to his kingdom, which is a kingdom of sin.

Since no one is exempt from this environment, all are under sin. The Jews under Roman rule made a case out of this; they are the one's whom the Law of God was entrusted. And they were to uphold the law by being obedient and doing what God required of them. But since the law was entrusted to them, they felt the law was applicable only to them and they were the only ones who could live a "righteous life."

Anyone outside the Jewish nation was considered a sinner. They, the outsiders, however, were looked upon as susceptible to this sinful environment and were indulging in sin in all mannerisms. In their life, the Jews proclaimed them to have hatred, jealousy, pride, adultery, and many more kinds of sins in their life.

However, the scripture tell us that all is under sin. Romans 3:9 says, *"What then? are we better than they? No, in no wise: for we have before proved both Jews and Gentiles, that they are all under sin."* In other words, all are subjected to a sinful life no matter what your nationality, your race, or your culture is. Therefore, the religious and non-religious are guilty before the Lord. That means no one is better than the other one and all "have come short of the glory of God."

This is why it is so important to fortify, strengthen one's faith and understanding of God's Word. The more one thirsts for and drinks His Word, the stronger he will become in resisting the temptations of Satan. No matter how strong your belief in Christ, your commitment to doing God's will, or your dedication to the task you are assigned, the temptation of Satan will still come after you, trying to get you to yield to what he is offering.

Though sometimes we all fall short of the glory of God by accepting the deal Satan is offering and yielding to the sin at hand, there is always a way back. The path to getting back came about when Jesus Christ shed His blood and gave up His life for our salvation.

Though we all are living in a sinful environment, it doesn't make us an automatic sinner. If you are in Christ, then you are able the make the right choice: which is not to yield to sin. 1 John 5:18 profoundly states, *"We know that whosoever is born of God sinneth not; but he that is begotten of God keepeth himself, and that wicked one toucheth him not."* Thus being born of God is the key to righteousness and not sinning. One may ask how do you become "born of God"? This can only happen by going through Jesus Christ our Savior.

Though all is under sin in a sinful environment, we must make sure that our life is saved by the salvation Jesus brought to the table for everyone. The first step in being saved from this sinful environment is to adhere to Romans 9:10-13: *"That if thou shalt confess with thy mouth the Lord Jesus, and shalt believe in thine heart that God hath raised him from the dead, thou shalt be saved. For with the heart man believeth unto righteousness; and with the mouth confession is made unto salvation. For the scripture saith, Whosoever believeth on him shall not be ashamed. For there is no difference between the Jew and the Greek: for the same Lord over all is rich unto all that call upon him. For whosoever shall call upon the name of the Lord shall be saved."* It is simple for anyone to win the war waged by Satan. All you need to do is truly confess your sin, believe what Jesus did, and walk in the spirit. The sin you face in your daily life will be repelled from you and not become a part of you.

The Savior

Who Died for Our Sins

Chapter 13

The Knowledge of Sin

Having a law is of the utmost importance to man. Simply because if there were no law, how would one know right from wrong, correct or incorrect, bad or good. The law is designed to be a guiding point for one in the appropriate direction. The law, like sin, is made up of choices. You can say yes or no whether you are going to adhere to it. Sin is a choice; you have the yes or no option. The law may be imposed upon a people, but it does not necessarily mean it is just, right, humane, correct or fair.

The definition of a law is a binding custom or practice of a community: a rule of conduct or action prescribed or formally recognized as binding or enforced by a controlling authority. (Merriam-Webster Dictionary Online).

There are two classes of laws: one human and the other is spiritual law. Human law is law that is made by man based up on his culture, his society, his desires, and his relationship with one another. It is an authority that is created where a superiority status to another is established. It is designed to only benefit man's desires and needs. It cultivates inequality and creates a superior power over others. This type of law can encompass right and wrong depending on what is applicable to what the society dictates. The aim is to satisfy man not God.

The other class of law is the spiritual one where the main goal and objective is to please God. Therefore, since the law of man refers only to man's ways, in the spiritual world, the Word of God is the guiding line. When laws made by man are properly observed, man is pleased. But when the Word of God is obeyed, it pleases God.

But the important revealing factor of a spiritual law is that it primarily makes known to man the enemy of God, which is sin that is orchestrated by Satan. As Romans 3:20 states, *"Therefore by the deeds of the law there shall no flesh be justified in his sight: for by the law is the knowledge of sin?"* The spiritual law (Word of God) reveals sin. It shows that man is subject to sin and the Word is a roadmap that assists in leading man away from his enemy's weapon and defeating Satan's device which is sin and whose objective is to devour all he can.

Sin is exemplified via the Word of God. It makes a distinction between what one is to do and not do. It gives you knowledge of sin, how it works, and how to defeat it in battle. It shows us where we go wrong.

Man is set apart via the Word of God, or moreover, he is justified. In the spiritual arena, one is either with God or Satan, in righteousness or unrighteousness, with love or hatred, with a sinful lifestyle, such as lust of the flush, the pride of life, or uncontrolled eye.

The Word of God is knowledge. It is needed in every aspect of life, spiritual, morally, financially, physically, etc. It is needed because its very fiber helps you to stand and use your knowledge of sin and how to fight it off and not allow it to come into our lives.

The Word of God is given through scripture in the Holy Bible, not on paper written by secular man. Thus, it is imperative that each and every one who believes in God and the death, burial, and resurrection of Jesus Christ establishes in his heart, mind, and soul the knowledge of God. Once this is established, one comes to believe in his mind and heart that he is open to receive the knowledge if instruction from God and how to apply His (Jesus) teaching to his daily life. Thus, he gains knowledge of the Word and understanding to help him become obedient to the Word of God.

It must be noted the when one gains knowledge of the law, the law does not provide salvation. That is only done through our lord and savior Jesus Christ. Once saved, it is important to obtain more knowledge of God and His Will. Hosea 4:6 says, *"My people are destroyed for the lack of knowledge: because thou has rejected knowledge, I will also reject thee, that thou shalt be no priest to me: seeing thou hast forgotten the law of thy God, I will also forget thy children."* The knowledge Hosea is speaking about is spiritual knowledge, not knowledge in general.

Developing knowledge of sin is predicated on one knowing the "law of thy God" (Hosea 4:6). One might ask, "How do I obtain the knowledge of the 'law of thy God'?" This knowledge can be obtained by following the five steps in getting to know God's Word: 1. One must **hear** the Word of God, 2. One must **read** the Word of God, 3. One must **study** the Word of God, 4. One must **meditate** on the Word of God, and 5. One must **do** the Word of God. By applying these steps, you surely will learn and gain knowledge of sin and how it is manifested. In addition to these five steps, one should pray for knowledge of sin.

Knowledge of sin is obtained no other way but through the Word of God. The Word of God tells us that sin can kill you. Therefore, it is of the utmost importance to be obedient to His Word and the commandments our Lord and Savior Jesus Christ gave us.

It is not only the lack of knowledge of sin that will destroy you, but also the knowledge of sin can do the same thing. This can be seen in the book of Genesis when God first made man. After man was made, God laid down the rules man had to abide by. Genesis

2:16-17 ESV) states, *"And the Lord God commanded the man, saying "You may surely eat of every tree on the garden, but of the tree of the knowledge of good and evil you shall not eat, for in the day that you eat of it you shall surely die."* This shows that man had knowledge of sin or rather evil (sin). Sin is evil. Yet, he disobeyed God's commandment and ate from the tree of knowledge. Thus, he was disobedient to God's Word. Having knowledge is good, but one must know how to apply knowledge.

As a result of this act by man, the stage was set for man to die here on this earth. Prior to this, man could have lived continuously. Thus, having knowledge of sin can make a world of difference to someone.

Where does this knowledge come from and how does it come about? This question can best be answered from Proverbs 2:6 (ESV) *"For the Lord Gives wisdom; from his mouth comes knowledge and understanding."* With these three things: wisdom, His mouth, and understanding in the spiritual arena, one will have no problem in overcoming and warding off sin attacks because of the knowledge he received via God. As you live by the Word of God, there will surely be victory in your life.

Chapter 14
Impute Sin

One thing all must remember is that a sin that is confessed is a sin forgiven. This is how it works in all sinful acts. God has promised He will forgive our sin if we confess it with our mouth. Note that it must be done verbally. It should not be done by written statement or sent by email. When you confess sin, God hears you. Isaiah 59:1 states, *"Behold, the Lord's hand is not shortened, that it cannot save; neither his ears heavy, thae it cannot hear."*

God cannot ignore sin because He hates it. He doesn't want this to be a part of His children's life because it cuts off the relationship He has with them. God does not tolerate sin no matter what the sin is and how it came about. Whenever one commits a sin, he is guilty of it. But the wonderful thing about God is that He will not hold it against you.

There are two methods by which God deals with sin. The first is that it is forgiven and forgotten once a confession of it is made and forgiveness asked. Once this is done, God takes the sin you have committed and throws it in the "sea of forgetfulness." In other words, He will not hold this against you, and it will not count as a merit toward you. This is what fortifies one's relationship with God. On the other hand, the second method God deals with sin is by providing the opportunity for repentance of the sin committed.

Many brothers and sisters repeat the same sin continuously. This continuous sin prevents a fervent relationship with God or if there is a relationship already established, it will destroy that relationship. The ultimate result of this lifestyle is that one will die with his sin unforgiven and separate himself from God eternally.

In the book of Romans Chapter 4 Verses 7 and 8 state" *"Blessed are they whose iniquities are forgiven, and whose sin are covered. Blessed is the man to whom the Lord will not impute sin."* In essence, what is said here is that God will not lay blame or hold your sin against you. You are separated from the sin, and it is cast away from your life.

It is so wonderful to have the grace of God at hand. The goodness of God is that no matter what kind of sin committed, He will forgive. Kind David, for example, was adulterous, a murder, a lying man, and much more, but God allowed him to experience the joy of forgiving, which brought a tremendous spiritual change in his life. The guilt David experienced after he had committed these sins affected his life at one point where he cried like a baby and tore off his clothes. But he learned how to seek forgiveness and the benefits of forgiveness. Psalm 103 shows why one should seek forgiveness and be open for His blessing:

"Bless the Lord, O my soul: and all that is within me, bless his holy name. Bless the Lord, O my soul, and forget not all his benefits: Who forgiveth all thine iniquities; who healeth all thy diseases; Who redeemeth thy life from destruction; who crowneth thee with lovingkindness and tender mercies; Who satisfieth thy mouth with good things; so that thy youth is renewed like the eagle's.

The Lord executeth righteousness and judgment for all that are oppressed. He made known his ways unto Moses, his acts unto the children of Israel. The Lord is merciful and gracious, slow to anger, and plenteous in mercy. He will not always chide: neither will he keep his anger forever. He hath not dealt with us after our sins; nor rewarded us according to our iniquities. For as the heaven is high above the earth, so great is his mercy toward them that fear him."

It is important to know sin can bring disaster to one's life and pave the way to join Satan in his kingdom for eternal damnation. But, living a life without sin has great benefits, not just here on earth but with a wonderful life in heaven with our Lord God and Jesus Christ forever, a life where there is no struggle, where you are not confronted with tribulations, which everyone on earth experiences.

As you repent of your sin, you can be assured He will not hold it against you once you have gone through the process of forgiveness.

A good example how sin is imputed is when the prophet Hosea was told to find him a wife of whoredom. This woman had committed many sins, but Hosea forgave her and accepted her as his wife. Even after a period of time of marriage, she left her husband and went to lay with other men. Hosea, having a heart of God, took her back in his home and forgave her.

That is the ways of God. It is by His grace that He will not remember our sin that has been forgiven, and it is by His mercy that He keeps His hand stretched out to us to save us from our sin.

Chapter 15
Death by Sin

It is known by everyone that everyone sooner or later will experience death. Death is the cessation of life in a body. There is nothing on earth that man can do to avoid this event. It can be a glorious or deplorable event. Glorious in the sense that death can be an extension of life full of perfect peace and assurance, or deplorable in the sense that there will be a life of eternal agony. There is life after death, and it depends where each individual prepares himself to go.

The factor that determines where one will go after death is sin. Sin is a killer. However, when looking at sin as a killer, one has to consider the aspects of death. Death comes in three forms: physical, spiritual, and eternal. One may say that the physical death is necessary for the spiritual or eternal death. However, one can depart from this earth without experiencing the physical; this is exemplified by the death of Elijah the prophet. 2 Kings 2:11 says, "*And it came to pass, as they still went on, and talked, that, behold, there appeared a chariot of fire, and horses of fire, and parted them both asunder; and Elijah went up by a whirlwind into heaven."* Even though this is not likely to happen, it is possible. God has the power to take us whichever way He so pleases.

Of all the three types of death, spiritual death leading to eternal death will cut off all or any relationship with an eternal life with God. Romans 5:12 states, *"Wherefore, as by one man sin entered into the world, and death by sin; and so death passed upon all men, for that all have sinned:"* Sin entered into this world via one man, Adam. Because of his disobedience, man throughout all generations has had to deal with sin. Sin has become an enemy of man simply because its intention is to cut off all of man's connection with God, and it does not want the best for you; Satan lives off evil.

When this separation happens, there is no eternal life in heaven. This separation can lead to an eternal life without God with Satan and his demons wherever they may be. Romans 20:10 explains what will happen for those who death is by sin: *"And the devil that deceived them was cast into the lake of fire and brimstone, where the beast and the false prophet are, and shall be tormented day and night for ever and ever."* However, Romans 21:8 is more descriptive and gives examples on who are the ones who all killed by sin. *"But the fearful, and unbelieving, and the abominable, and murderers, and whoremongers, and sorcerers, and idolaters, and all liars, shall have their part in the lake which burneth with fire and brimstone: which is the second death."*

Adam's sin established the death of man. If Adam had not sinned, there would not have been death as we know it. When God created man, He created him for His enjoyment and His pleasure, but when the created man violated Him, man's existence became dependent on his services rendered to God as a servant, proving himself to be worthy to our God. He, therefore, can achieve this by being obedient to God's Word.

No one wants to die, but it is inevitable. Therefore, it is imperative for one to live the life God has so prescribed for him. A life of obedience to His Word is required, so that there will be life after death in a marvelous world with Him in eternity. But one must be willing to carry out the will of God, serving Him in every capacity of one's life: spiritually, physically, morally, and financially. We should serve God as a "Man of God." This is what some of the great servants, believers of God, were called in the Bible, which sets an example for us. Timothy was called a man of God. This title was given to Moses (Deuteronomy 33:1), David (Nehemiah 12:24), Elijah (1Kings 17:18) and Elisha (2 Kings 4:7).

Scripture tells us that all have sinned and come short of the glory of God. But to avoid a death of sin, seek forgiveness from God, repent and believe. Then, you will inherit the kingdom of God.

Capacity to Sin: Volume III

Chapter 16

Law and Sin

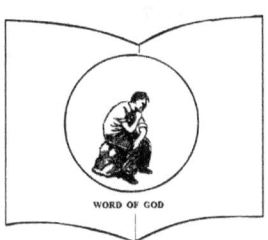

Sin existed before the law was given. The first law was given to man via Moses, which is known as the Ten Commandments. And, these laws are just alive today as they were then. The law can be found in Exodus 20 and is stated as follows:

Ten Commandments
1. Thou shalt have no other gods before me.
2. Thou shalt not make unto thee any graven image, or any likeness of anything that is in heaven above, or that is in the earth beneath, or that is in the water under the earth:
3. Thou shalt not take the name of the Lord thy God in vain;
4. Remember the Sabbath day, to keep it holy.
5. Honor thy father and thy mother:
6. Thou shalt not kill.
7. Thou shalt not commit adultery.
8. Thou shalt not steal.
9. Thou shalt not bear false witness against thy neighbor.
10. Thou shalt not covet thy neighbor's house, thou shalt not covet thy neighbor's wife, nor his manservant, nor his

maidservant, nor his ox, nor his ass, nor any thing that is thy neighbor's.

Breaking these laws are just a few of the sins that Christians today can commit. This applies to all Christians today as well as yesterday. However, these laws help us learn more about God's holiness and can weld our bond in our relationship to Him and being obedient to Him. It set us apart for Him.

The laws came after sin. Sin was in the world before the law. Romans 5:13 states, *"For until the law sin was in the world: but sin is not imputed when there is no law."* The Quest Study Bible put it this way, in Romans 5:13: *"To be sure, sin was in the world before the law was given, but sin is not charged against anyone's account where there is no law."* In other words, even before the law, sin and death exercised power over all mankind. From the time of Adam to the time of Moses, man did not sin by breaking the law, but by the falling of their countenance or perhaps with a wroth spirit as Cain, Adam's son portrayed.

Between that time of Adam and Moses, there was sin. Everyone sinned. Why? Because it became a part of man's nature, thanks to Adam. The next sin of man discussed in the Bible was when Adam's son Cain sinned before God by murdering his brother. The power of death in many aspects was and is over man, which means everyone will meet a physical death sooner or later.

Sin and death are contrasted. Death will come, but not necessarily in the spiritual aspect of death. Spiritually, one can beat death thanks to our lord and savior Jesus Christ. Jesus came into this world to save it (man). John 3:16-18 says, *"For God so loved the world, that he gave his only begotten Son, that whosoever believeth in him should not perish, but have everlasting life. For God sent not his Son into the world to condemn the world; but that the world through him might be saved. He that believeth on him is not condemned: but he that believeth not is condemned already, because he hath not believed in the name of the only begotten Son of God."*

Chapter 17
Sin Reigned unto Death

When one sins and allows it to become perpetual, sin reigns in his life. Reign is a period of time which someone is in charge or a period of time during which someone or something is the best or most powerful. This is the form that sin takes in one's life if it is not defeated or cast out of one's life. Sin can be the master that will determine one's destiny.

When sin reigns in someone's life, it is like a king of a nation or a dictator. It makes all the rules you are to follow in daily life. However, one generally will become complacent with life without knowing the devastation and cruelty of sin's consequences or its end results. Sin is like a leach. It doesn't matter whom it attaches itself to as long as it can suck the blood out of you; if this process continues there will be no blood left in the body. The body will be subject to destruction for the lack of its life source (The Word of God).

As we look at the reign of sin, there is another side of the coin. On the other side, we have something that is more powerful than sin.

As a matter of fact is can cancel out sin all together. This is none other than the reign of grace; it is mighty. Grace reigns through righteousness. As Romans 5:21 states, *"That as sin hath reigned unto death, even so might grace reign through righteousness unto eternal life by Jesus Christ our Lord."*

The reign of grace came about with the coming of Jesus Christ. With Christ our Lord, the end result is eternal life with Him and without destruction or torture eternally. As one recognizes and receives grace via our God, it manifests itself as forgiveness. This means sin is canceled out or propitiated via the death of Jesus Christ. Jesus came to this world to save the world and not to destroy it. He came to take us away for the reign of sin in our life.

As the mighty grace reigns through righteousness, there is peace, and everyone has access to God's grace. Through grace, there is hope, there is love, and there is the availability of the Holy Spirit to guide you through life until the time comes for your eternal stay with Jesus in heaven.

The reign of sin started when Adam disobeyed God. This reign of sin was until death. As stated in Romans 5:14: *"Nevertheless death reigned from Adam to Moses, even over them that had not sinned after the similitude of Adam's transgression, who is the figure of him that was to come."* As sin reigned, it mastery came to an end via Jesus Christ. Again, through Christ, grace was "born." Therefore, as the shackle of sin is broken, it is up to every individual, whether he wants to walk the road of death brought on by sin or with grace brought on by righteousness.

One must use the Word of God to break the hold of sin. Romans 6:12 says, *"Let not sin therefore reign in your mortal body, that ye should obey it in the lusts thereof."* When sin reigns, it gives you a mindset to see only things here on earth as worthwhile. One cannot see that there is life after death (physical). Only the lust of your flesh is important in life. However, this is temporary. The flesh withers away, but there is eternal life after death, through living an obedient and righteous life through Christ.

Chapter 18
Continue in Sin

The biggest challenge in sin is sinning in a perpetual state. This is when one who sins continues to indulge in his sinful acts, whether it is the same sin or a different one. One needs help because there is a problem moving out of the sin's arena. As long as one is on the team, he will play. Even when one is on the bench, he is still a part of the team of sin. In other words, if you continue to have sinful thoughts, then you are a player. Thus, the grace of God can help resolve this problem.

We are not under the law anymore but under grace. Grace is the undeserving favor we receive from God. Everyone can receive grace. It is a gift from God with no strings attached. As a matter of fact, it is not wrapped like one usually receives a gift. It is given to one from the love from God. It cannot be earned because what drives grace is God's love for us.

Salvation is a product of grace. This is the gift that causes one to be saved. It is all from God. Ephesians 3:8-9 say, *"For by grace are ye saved through faith; and that not of yourselves: it is the gift of*

God: Not of works, lest any man should boast." This is the first thing grace does- it saves. However, once one is saved, he is still subjected to errors via sin. Matthew 22:29 tells us what Jesus said about errors. *"Jesus answered and said unto them, Ye do err, not knowing the scriptures, nor the power of God.* But Grace keeps on working and is always available. It is available because if one happens to sin, God's grace and mercy will give you the opportunity to be forgiven and eradicate this sin.

As one keeps on living, there is the capacity to sin. No one is immune to sin. Life is a struggle, and as we struggle against the prince of darkness and principalities, we are subject to sinful acts. When/if it does happen, then one needs to seek forgiveness from God and repent. God's grace is always available to provide this.

Most people/believers understand the principle of grace and forgiveness. By the grace of God, one is forgiven for his sins. But one cannot think he can take the advantage of God's grace. This is done by intentionally sinning and thinking God's grace is there to take care of it as the sin is repeated.

One tries to take advantage of grace by committing a sin over and over and asking for forgiveness from God. When this happens, it opens the door to use up the grace God has for you. Hebrews 10:26 states, "For *if we sin willfully after that we have received the knowledge of the truth, there remaineth no more sacrifice for sins."*

There is an abundance of grace, but grace is applied by God through looking at the heart. This abundance of grace is not for evil doers.

One continues in sin simply because there is no repentance; therefore there is enough grace to take care of all of the sinful acts of sinners through forgiveness. But, if there is a lack of repentance, then the effect is keeping on doing what is wrong in God's eyes and He will surely cut one off from the mercy and grace God has made available for everyone. If one continues, then he will have to suffer the consequences, which are not favorable.

God wants all to be prosperous, victorious, and sin free in life, to enjoy all of the fruits of life. The fruits of life are stated in Galatians 5:22-25: *"But the fruit of the Spirit is love, joy, peace, longsuffering, gentleness, goodness, faith, meekness, temperance: against such there is no law. And they that are Christ's have crucified the flesh with the affections and lusts. If we live in the Spirit, let us also walk in the Spirit."*

The key in not continuing in sin but abiding in what verse 25 says: *"If we live in the Spirit, let us also walk in the Spirit."* By doing this, sinful habits can be canceled out and cut off from one's life in such a way that one's life will be victorious; it is glorifying God for who He is in his life.

To continue in sin will cut out all the blessings God has in store for you- you will not receive His "benefits." Psalms 103:1-2 state, *"Bless the Lord, O my soul: and all that is within me, bless his holy name. Bless* forgiveness. Romans 6:1 states, *"What shall we say then? Shall we continue in sin, that grace may abound?"* The "New Living Translation states Romans 6:1 this way: *"Well then, should we keep on sinning so that God can show us more and more of his wonderful grace?"*

God's grace is abundance, but it is not a license to sin. It is to provide salvation and the road to righteousness. Those who have this type of attitude will continue to sin without any remorse. When one does this, he is sinning away his mercy. This will cause the door of heaven to shut up on him. You can correlate this attitude with one of a hypocrite.

It is important to know God's grace is not only abundant, but it is also full of mercy. As you continue in sin because grace is abundant, you will cut off your relationship with God. Then what will happen? Hebrews 10:26 gives a good explanation; *"For if we sin wilfully after that we have received the knowledge of the truth, there remaineth no more sacrifice for sins, Thus the Lord, O my soul, and forget not all his benefits:"*

Chapter 19

Dead to Sin

There is no direct proportionality between God's grace and sin. That means if one continues to sin, he can take advantage of His grace, and he would think that he receives the pleasure or gratitude from the sin he committed. Sin can be defeated. Once defeated, every time sin rears its ugly head, you can snip it off by resisting the devil and watching him flee from you.

But the key in defeating sin is to become "dead to sin." This way sin is not allowed to take part in one's life. There are no grounds for it to plant its roots. One can walk in righteousness as God wants all to do and honor Him for keeping you. Christ made it possible for us to die to sin. This means even though sin is all around us, our relationship to it is dead. Therefore, sin no longer has authority over us. Sin such as scornfulness, sexual immorality, and stealing are blocked out due to one's death to sin.

Romans 6:2 states, *"God forbid, How shall, we, that are dead to sin. Live any longer therein?"* One cannot continue to ask for grace or forgiveness in sin that is perpetuated; that is, continued as it is a daily routine without thought to its consequences. Even if one continues sinning and seeking forgiveness, it is not the full process of forgiveness. When forgiveness is asked, one is or should be focused on getting sin completely out of his life. Seeking forgiveness and continuing to sin is not a description of one who has died to sin.

One who is dead to sin cannot live a sinful life because that relationship is broken that he once had with sin, whereas sin was their motive, pleasure, objective and way of life is buried and stripped from his lifestyle. He seeks righteousness via our lord and Savior Jesus Christ.

Dead to sin means sin is around you but you have no use for it. When it gases up and tries to drive itself into your life, you close the door and do not let it in. You will keep confessing the Word of God to keep this door locked. Even when it knocks on your door, you will give it no thought of opening it.

Jesus Christ made it possible to be dead to sin through His death, burial and resurrection. This was done so that we can be alive to God, thus living the type of life God wants us to live. Jesus came into this world so we may live, have life more abundantly, being upright and free from the snares of sin. John 10:10 says, *"I am the door: by me if any man enter in, he shall be saved, and shall go in and out, and find pasture. The thief cometh not, but for to steal, and to kill, and to destroy: I am come that they might have life, and that they might have it more abundantly."* Sin is deadly; it is the weapon than will keep you from having eternal life with our God and Jesus Christ.

Sin not only keeps you from eternal life, there are other repercussions of sins while you are living life here on this earth. First, it puts your in direct violation of God's purpose; He did not put you here on the earth to sin. He put you here to please Him, worship Him and to carry out His commands and will. Sin impedes this or becomes a road block in you carrying out God's plan. After all, all have a choice on which path to take.

Secondly, sin can destroy all of the moral fabric one has in life; immorality is a sin as pointed out in Jeremiah 3:9: *"Because Israel's immorality mattered so little to her, she defiled the land and committed adultery with stone and wood"* (NIV Quest Study Bible) and Jude 1:4 *"For certain individuals whose condemnation was written about long ago have secretly slipped in among you, there are ungodly people, who pervert the grace of our God into a license for immorality and deny Jesus Christ our only Sovereign and Lord"* (NIV Quest Study Bible). Living a life without morals, sin can paint your life as a picture where one cannot see any wrong in it. Sin can inflate your mind with deception; this will happen as a repercussion of sin if one is not dead to it.

Thirdly, not being dead to sin, the repercussions of sin can create a selfish instrument that a Christian can use to try and take advantage of God. This is done by using God's forgiveness and grace to support his indulgence in sin. That is, he knows His grace and forgiveness is always available for one to use to wash away the sinful act and to forgive. However, grace and forgiveness are great but they can become futile to one if he does not repent. As a matter of fact, this is rather an insult to God. Because you use what He has provided for you, but you turn around and do the same and continue in your sin. Scripture says we are susceptible to err. When this happens, one needs to know the tools and processes that can be used to set the record straight.

Once one is dead to sin, he no longer allows sin to enter into his live. He strives to live a life of righteousness via the faith in our Lord. When Satan comes to knock on your door, you have the strength and stamina to not reach for the door knob and let him in.

This takes a lot of strength to be able to resist the devil. But it is through Jesus that this can be manifested. Thus, this manifestation depends on what steps one must first take.

There is not better guide to accomplish this than as described in Galatians 2:20 which states, *"I have been crucified with Christ. It is no longer I who live, but Christ who lives in me. And the life I now live in the flesh I live by faith in the Son of God, who loved me and gave himself for me."* To be "crucified with Christ" is to become dead to sin.

Luke 9:23-24 makes it even clearer what one should do to become dead to sin; it states, *"And he said to all, If anyone would come after me, let him deny himself and take up his cross daily and follow me. For whoever would save his life will lose it, but whoever loses his life for my sake will save it."*

Chapter 20

Freed from Sin

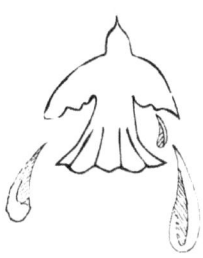

The origin of sin was from the beginning of man. It did not come into existence until shortly after man's creation, namely the deadly act that Adam committed. Sin came by way of one man, and it trickled down through men from generation to generation. But on the other hand, sin was put to death by one man, Jesus Christ.

The world before the coming of Jesus was at a loss because the sin in it was destroying man because of his way of dealing with it had become no longer effective. Man had proved himself to be ineffective in his method of eradicating sin in his life. There were law and sacrifices in effect, but that was not enough to free him from his sin. He would sin and turn around and sin again. Sin was like a bouncing ball in his life.

God saw the need to give the opportunity for man to be free from sin. God's plan was to use His only begotten son to accomplish this task. He therefore allowed his Son, Jesus Christ, to take on the form of man on earth to liberate man from his enemy: sin. Christ came to save man as stated in John 3:16-17" *"For God so loved the world, that he gave his only begotten Son, that whosoever believeth in him should not perish, but have everlasting life. For God sent not his Son into the world to condemn the world; but that the world through him might be saved."* To be saved from sin is to be freed from sin. In order for this to happen, it was divinely necessary for Jesus Christ's death to take place as it did on the cross at Calvary.

When Jesus was crucified, buried and raised from the dead, that was the door to freedom from sin. That was the only way that man could be saved or freed:

Romans 6: 5-11 says: *"For if we have been planted together in the likeness of his death, we shall be also in the likeness of his resurrection: Knowing this, that our old man is crucified with him, that the body of sin might be destroyed, that henceforth we should not serve sin. For he that is dead is freed from sin. Now if we be dead with Christ, we believe that we shall also live with him: Knowing that Christ being raised from the dead dieth no more; death hath no more dominion over him. For in that he died, he died unto sin once: but in that he liveth, he liveth unto God. Likewise reckon ye also yourselves to be dead indeed unto sin, but alive unto God through Jesus Christ our Lord."*

Christ is the only man to walk this earth without sin. He was tempted by Satan just like all of us. We are tempted by the same devil that tempted him. Of course, He did not yield. As we are tempted today, we should take the same stand as Jesus did. Just say no to the devil.

Christ's death is a likeness to our life, where we can be free from sin because of what He did for us. That means we have freedom from sin. If one fervently believes what Christ did and lives a life like Christ, then that door of freedom is available. Available because Christ's death opened the door so man can be freed from sin. But, it is up to each believer to walk through this door of freedom.

You are free from sin because you are dead to sin; that means nowhere in your life is there room for sin to become a part of your life. Dead means there is no life; thus, it cannot live in your saved body. When you are dead in sin, it means you have made a divinely, dedicated decision to walk away from sin no matter what the circumstances are.

Free from sin means one will not commit sin when sin entices him. The power of that resistance to not yield to sin is the mighty powerful spirit in you, Jesus Christ. Zechariah 4:6 says, *"Not by might nor by power, but by Spirit, says the LORD Almighty."* With Christ in you, you are filled with the Holy Spirit whom Christ left to all who wants to receive Him (Holy Spirit). If you allow Him to guide you, you will not sin or yield to Satan's temptations; you will not let lust of the flesh, the lust of the eyes, and the pride of life cause you to sin. 1 John 2:16 says, *"For all that is in the world, the lust of the flesh, and the lust of the eyes, and the pride of life, is not of the Father, but is of the world."*

Capacity to Sin: Volume III

Theme Verses

Chapter 1
Matthew 18:21 *"Then came Peter to him, and said, Lord, how oft shall my brother sin against me, and I forgive him? till seven times?"*

Chapter 2
John 1:29 *"The next day John seeth Jesus coming unto him, and saith, Behold the Lamb of God, which taketh away the sin of the world."*

Chapter 3
John 5: 14 *"Afterward Jesus findeth him in the temple, and said unto him, Behold, thou art made whole: sin no more, lest a worse thing come unto thee."*

Chapter 4
John 8:7 *"So when they continued asking him, he lifted up himself, and said unto them, He that is without sin among you, let him first cast a stone at her."*

Chapter 5
John 8:34 *"Jesus answered them, Varily, Varily, I say unto you, Whosoever committeth sin is the servant of sin."*

Chapter 6
John 9:2 *"And his disciples asked him, saying, Master, who did sin, this man, or his parents, that he was born blind?"*

Chapter 7
John 9:14 *"Jesus said unto them, If ye were blind, ye should have no sin: but now ye say, We see; therefore your sin remaineth."*

Chapter 8
John 15:22 *"If I had not come and spoken unto them, they had not had sin: but now they have no cloke for their sin."*

Chapter 9
John 16:7-8 *"Nevertheless I tell you the truth; It is expedient for you that I go away: for if I go not away, the comforter will not come unto you. And when he is come, he will reprove the world of sin and of righteousness, and of judgement: of sin, because they believer not on me; of righteousness, because I go to my Father, and ye see me no more; of judgement, because the prince of this world is judged"*

Chapter 10
John 19:11 *"Jesus answered, Thou couldest have no power at all against me, except it were given thee from above: therefore he that delivered me unto thee hath the greater sin."*

Chapter 11
Act 7:60 *"And he kneeled down, and cried with a loud voice, Lord, lay not this sin to their charge. And when he had said this, he fell asleep."*

Chapter 12
Romans3:9 *"What then? are we better than they? No, in no wise: for we have before proved both Jews and Gentiles, that they are all under sin;"*

Chapter 13
Romans 3:20 *"Therefore by the deeds of the law there shall no flesh be justified in his sight: for by the law is the knowledge of sin?"*

Chapter 14
Romans4:7-8 *"Blessed are they whose iniquities are forgiven, and whose sin are covered. Blessed is the man to whom the Lord will not impute sin."*

Chapter 15
Romans5:12 *"Wherefore, as by one man sin entered into the world, and death by sin; and so death passed upon all men, for that all have sinned."*

Chapter 16
Romans5:13 *"For until the law sin was in the world: but sin is not imputed when there is no law."*

Chapter 17
Romans5:21 *"That as sin hath reigned unto death, even so might grace reign through righteousness unto eternal life by Jesus Christ our Lord."*

Chapter 18
Romans6:1 *"What shall we say then? Shall we continue in sin, that grace may abound?"*

Chapter 19
Romans 6:2 *"God forbid, How shall, we, that are dead to sin. Live any longer therein."*

Chapter 20
Romans 6: 5-11 *"For if we have been planted together in the likeness of his death, we shall be also in the likeness of his resurrection: Knowing this, that our old man is crucified with him, that the body of sin might be destroyed, that henceforth we should not serve sin. For he that is dead is freed from sin. Now if we be dead with Christ, we believe that we shall*

also live with him: Knowing that Christ being raised from the dead dieth no more; death hath no more dominion over him. For in that he died, he died unto sin once: but in that he liveth, he liveth unto God. Likewise reckon ye also yourselves to be dead indeed unto sin, but alive unto God through Jesus Christ our Lord."

Rayford J. Elliott

List of Commonly Committed Sins and their Causes

*Bible verses used from ESV, NIV, KJV, and Topical Bible.

abandonment	Psalm 34:18; Psalm 27:10
abduction	Deuteronomy 24:7
abhorring judgment	Leviticus 26:43-44; Romans 2:1 Psalm 26:5
abomination	Leviticus 20:13
abortion	Exodus 20:21-25
abusiveness	2 Peter 1:4
abhorrence of holy things	Act 2:33
accusation	Jude 1:9
adulterous lust	Matthew 5:27-28
adultery	Proverb 6:24-29; Proverb 6:32
afflicting others	Isaiah 58:1-14
aggravation	Genesis 2:24
agitation	Proverb 12:25
aiding and abetting sin	Colossians 3:12-17; 2 John 1:10
alcoholism	Galatians 5:21
all unrighteousness	1 John 1:9
anger	James 1:20
animosity	Ephesians 4:32
anxiety	Peter 5:6-7
apprehension	2 Thessalonians 1:1-12
argumentativeness	2 Timothy 2:15
arrogance	1Samuel 2:3
assaults	2 Samuel 13:1-39
astrology	Deuteronomy 28:9-12
atheism	Psalm 14:1
avariciousness	1 Timothy 6:9
Baal worship	2 Kings 17:16

backbiting	Proverbs 16:28; Romans 16:17:18
backsliding	2 Corinthians 13:5; Proverbs 14:14
bad attitude	Psalm 104:19
bad language	Ephesians 4:29
bearing false witness	Proverbs 19:5
big talk	Hebrews 10:25; Proverbs 10:19
being a workaholic	Proverbs 23:4; Proverbs 13:11 Ecclesiastes 3:1-22
being too quick to speak	Proverbs 17:28
believing lies of the enemy	1 John 4:1; 2 Corinthians 11:13-15
belittling	Isaiah 55:8-9; Romans 15:1-33
bereavement	1 Thessalonians 4:13; John 5:28
betraying Jesus	Matthew 27:3; John 13:21
bickering	Philippians 2:14; Psalm 37:1-40
bigotry	Galatians 3:28; 1 Peter 2:1-25
bitterness	Ephesians 4:31-32; Proverbs 15:1
black magic	Deuteronomy 18:9-14 Hebrews 13:8-9
blackmail	1 Corinthians 6:9-11
blaspheming the Holy Spirit	Matthew 12:31-32; Mark 3:29
boastfulness	Matthew 6:1-2; James 4:6
boisterousness	Exodus 23:1 1; Corinthians 6:9-10
bowing down to images	1 Timothy 2:5; Exodus 20:4-5
bragging	Matthew 6:1-34; Jude 1:16 Jeremiah 9:23
brainwashing	Philippians 4:8; John 14:16
breaking God's commands	John 14:23-24; John 14:15
breaking God's covenants	Luke 22:30; 1 Corinthians 11:25
breaking covenants w/others	Hebrews 13:4; Genesis 2:14
bribery	Exodus 23:8; Proverb 15:27 Proverb 17:23
brutality	Matthew 10:17-18; Revelation 20:4
burning incense to gods	Leviticus 10:1-2; Isaiah 1:13
calamity	Isaiah 45:7; Job 2:10

carelessness	2 Timothy 2:15; Joshua 1:8
cares & riches of this world	Matthew 6:24; 2 Corinthians 8:9
carnality	1 Corinthians 3:3; Romans 8:6
casting God away	1 John 4:1; 1 Chronicles 10:13-14
causing disagreements	Colossians 2:1-23
causing distress	2 Thessalonians 2:1-7
	Colossians 3:1-25
causing division	Romans 16:17-18; 2 Timothy 6:3-5
causing fear	John 14:27; 1 Peter 5:8
causing men to err	John 10:1-42; 1 Peter 1:22
causing offense	1 Corinthians 8:1-13
	2 Timothy 3:16
causing poor to fail	Luke 14:12-14; Luke 12:23
changing truth to lies	John 8:44; Ephesians 4:25
chanting of charms	Deuteronomy 18:9-12
	1 Corinthians 13:1-13
cheating	James 4:17; Hebrews 13:4
come against God's anointed	1 Samuel 24:6; 1 John 2:27
complaining	Philippians 2:14; Ephesians 4:29
complacency anti God's will	Proverb 1:23
	Hebrews 5:11-12
conceit	Romans 12:16; Jeremiah 9:23
	Proverb 26:12
concupiscence	Colossians 3:5; 1 Corinthians 13:8
condemnation	Romans8:1; Romans 2:1-29
condemning the just	Ephesians 4:32; 1 Peter 3:8
causing conflict	Ephesians 4:32; 1 Peter 3:8
confrontation	Matthew 18:15:20; Galatians 6:1
confusion	2 Timothy 2:7; 1 Corinthians 14:33
conjuration	1 Timothy 4:1; 2 John 1:9-11
conspiring against God	Romans13:1-14 Exodus 23:1
consulting wizards, psychics	Leviticus 19:31
	1 Chronicles 10:13-14
contempt	Romans 14:1-23

contention	Proverbs 3:30
controlling	2 Peter 1:5-8
conniving	Proverb 6:16-19; Exodus 20:16
compulsiveness	1 Corinthians 9:27
contentiousness	1 Corinthians 11:16
contesting and resisting God	1 Timothy 3:1-7; Romans1:19
corruption	2 Peter 2:19; 1 Thessalonians 5:22
counterfeiting Christian work	2 Corinthians 11:13-15; John 8:44
covering sin	Romans6:33; Proverbs 28:13
coveting	Exodus 20:17; Deuteronomy 5:22
covetousness	1 Timothy 6:6-11
cravenness	Proverbs 23:31
criticalness	Colossians 3:12-14
crookedness	Proverb 11:3; 2 Corinthians 4:4
cruelty	Proverb 12:10; Mark 9:43
using crystals	Acts 8:9-13
cursing God	Matthew 10:32-33
	Matthew 12:31:32
cursing	Ephesians 4:29; Ephesians 5:4
dealing treacherously	Romans 7:3; Hebrews 12:13
deceit	Proverbs 20:17; Psalm 101:17
deception	Galatians 6:7-8; Proverbs 10:9
defamation	Titus 3:1-2
defeatism	Ephesians 6:10-18
defiantness	Genesis 3:1-24
defiling	Leviticus 15:31; Numbers 6:9
degrading	Romans 1:24
dejection	Proverb 29:23
demon consciousness	Acts 16:16-18; Matthew 9:32-33
demon worship	Ephesians 6:10-13; Psalm 106:37
deny Jesus, His resurrection	Matthew 10:33
dependencies	1 Thessalonians 4:12; Leviticus 21:3
depravity	Romans 1:29; 2 Peter 2:19
desecration	Ezekiel 7:22; Deuteronomy 21:23

desires of this world	Colossians 3:5; Romans 12:2
despair	Isaiah 19:9; Isaiah 61:3
despising God	1 Samuel 2:30; 2 Samuel 12:9
despitefulness	Leviticus 20:13; Leviticus 18:22
despondency	Galatians 6:9; Revelation 21:4
deviousness	Proverb 2:16; Proverb 14:2
disagreements	Ephesians 4:31-5:2; Acts 15:36
disbelief	Mark 9:24; 2 Timothy 4:3-4
discord	Proverb 6:16-19; Esther 1:18
discrediting	2 Peter 1:21; 2 Timothy 3;16-17
discouragement	Exodus 6:9; Jeremiah 19:11 Exodus 6:9
disdain	Proverb 23:22; Romans 13:1-7
disgust	Ezekiel 23:17; Ezekiel 23:18
dishonesty	Colossians 3:9-10; Proverb 20:17 Exodus 20:16
disobedience	Deuteronomy 28:15; Hebrews 2:2
disorderly	2 Thessalonians 3:6; Romans 16:17
disputing	1 Timothy 2:8; Jude 1:9
disrespectfulness	1 Corinthians 15:33; Esther 1:18
disruptive	1 John 2:15; Ephesians 4:29
dissension	Proverb 6:14; Proverbs 15:18 Romans 13:13
distantness	Deuteronomy 30:4; Matthews 25:41
distrust	2 Timothy 3:16; John 13:35
division	1 Corinthians 1:10-13; Luke 11:17
divorce	Deuteronomy 24:1;1 Corinthians 7:15
domineering	Galatians 3:28; 1 Timothy 2:12
double-talking	1 Peter 5:8; 2 Corinthians 10:5 Proverbs 6:12-16
double mindedness	James 1:6-8; James 4:8
doubt	Proverbs 3:5-8; James 1:6
dread	Deuteronomy 7:21; John 14:1
drug abuse	1 Corinthians 6:19-201

	Corinthians 3:17
drunkenness	Proverbs 20:1; Ephesians 5:18
duplicity	Proverbs 6:16-19; Romans 12:17-21
	Exodus 20:16
drinking blood	Genesis 9:304; Acts 15:20
eating blood	Deuteronomy 12:33
eating unclean food	Acts 10:14
effeminate behavior	Deuteronomy 6:9; Hebrews 13:4
egotism	Philippians 2:1-10; John 5:31
enchantment	Numbers 23:23; Leviticus 19:23
enlarged imaginations	2 Corinthians 10:5
	Revelation 22:1-21
enter unrighteous agreements	Hosea 10:4
envy (produced by lust)	Job 5:2; Proverbs 3:31; 23:17
escaping	1 Corinthians 10:13; Luke 21:36
	Acts 2:40
evil hearts & imaginations	2 Thessalonians 3:2; Romans 6:23
exasperation	Ephesians 4:1-3; Matthew 5:40
	Proverbs 12:156
extortion	Leviticus 6:4; Ecclesiastes 7:7
	Isaiah 33:15
failure in duty	Genesis 38:8; Acts 23:1 1
	Corinthians 7:3
failure to glorify God	Psalm 69:12, 86:12; Romans 15:9
falsehood	Job 21:34; Psalm 119:163
	1 John 4:6
fantasizing	James 1:14-15; 2 Timothy 2:22
fault finding	John 7:24; Matthew 7:1-5
fear	2 Timothy 1:7; 1 John 4:18
fear of disapproval	2 Kings 8:19; Nehemiah 6:16
	Proverbs 3:32
fear of man	Proverb 29:25
fetishes	Romans 7:8; James 1:14
	2 Peter 2:10

fighting	Proverb 28:25; Matthew 18:15 Galatians 5:15
flattery	Proverbs 29:5; Job 32:21-22
foolishness	1 Corinthians 1:18, 1:23
folly	Job 42:8; Palm 69:5
forcefulness	Matthew 11:12; 2 Corinthians 10:10
fornication	1 Corinthians 7:2; 1 Corinthians 6:18
fortune telling	Leviticus 19:3 1 Deuteronomy 18:10-12
fraud	Luke 16:10-13; Proverbs 20:17 Jeremiah 10:14
fretting	1 Peter 5:5-7; 1 Peter 3:3-4
frustrations	2 Samuel 13:2; Nehemiah 4:15
fury	Job 40:11; Proverb 22:8 Genesis 27:44
giving offense	Genesis 20:16
gloominess	Zephaniah 1:15; Daniel 12:1
gluttony	Proverbs 23:2; Philippians 3:19 1 Corinthians 10:31
gossip	Proverbs 11:13, 20:19, 26:20
greed	Matthew 23:25; Luke 12:15
grieving	Nehemiah 8:10; 8:11 Ephesians 4:30
grumbling	Exodus 16:7; Numbers 17:10 John 6:43
guilt	Hosea 13:16; John 9:41; Hosea 5:15
harlotry	Nahum 3:4; Jeremiah 13:27; Hosea 5:4
harshness	Malachi 3:13; 2 Corinthians 13:10
hating God	Exodus 20:5
hating	Titus 3:3; Jude 1:23
haughtiness	Jeremiah 48:29
high-minded	1 Corinthians 1:19
homosexuality	1 Corinthians 6:9; Leviticus 18:22

hopeless	Isaiah 57:10
horoscopes	Leviticus 19:31; 1 John 4:1
human sacrifice	Deuteronomy 18:20
hypocrisy	Matthew 23:28; 1 Peter 2:1
idleness	2 Thessalonians 3:6; Proverbs 31:27
idle words, deeds, & actions	Matthew 12:36-37; Proverbs 18:8
idolatries	Jeremiah 14:14; 1 Corinthians 10:14 Colossians 3:5
ignorance	Ephesian 4:18; 1 Timothy 1:13
ill will	Deuteronomy 15:9
inhumanity	1 John 3:15
imaginations	2 Corinthians 10:5 Isaiah 65:2, 66:18
immorality	Jeremiah 3:9; Jude 1:4
impatience	James 5:7-8; Galatians 5:22 Colossians 1:11
impetuousness	Habakkuk 1:6
imprudence	Proverbs 14:8, 14:15
impurity	Leviticus 15:19; Zechariah 13:1
inadequacy	2 Corinthians 12:9; Philippians 1:20
incest	Leviticus 18:6-18 Deuteronomy 27:23
incitement	Proverbs 29:11
indifferences	Revelation 3:15-16 Matthew 11:16-17
inflating	Matthew 7:1; John 11:26
inflexibility	Philippians 4:1-23
inhospitality	Ezekiel 16:49-50; Genesis 19:5
iniquity in your heart	Psalm 25:11; 51:9
injustice	Micah 6:8; Exodus 23:7
insolence	Titus 3:2; Proverbs 15:1
intemperance	Proverbs 23:29-35; 2 Timothy 1:7
intentional sins	Hebrews 10:26
intimidation	Nehemiah 6:13, 14, 19

intolerances	2 Samuel 12:7
intellectualism, sophisticated	1 Timothy 6:20; 1 Corinthians 1;27
inventing sin	James 1:4; Acts 2:28
inventing evil	Romans 1:24-32; Psalm 55:15
inward wickedness	Ephesians 6:12
irrationality	Romans1:20; John 4:24
irreverence	Nehemiah 5:15; Jeremiah 44:10
jealousy	Exodus 34:14; Acts 7:9
being judgmental	Luke 6:37; John 12:48
justifying the wicked	Proverbs 11:1
kidnapping	Deuteronomy 24:7
killing	1 Samuel 19:5
lack of self-control	1 Corinthians 7:9
lawlessness	1 John 3:4; James 4:17
lasciviousness	Proverbs 2:16-18
laziness	Proverbs 12:24; Proverbs 19:16
lesbianism	Romans 1:27-27
levitation	Isaiah 60:1, 60:8
lewdness	Ephesians 5:5; 1 Corinthians 6:9-10
lying	Proverbs 12:22; 1 John 2:4
loathing	Psalm 119:158
longing for sin	1 Peter 2:1-25; 1 Timothy 2:1-15
loneliness	Psalm 25:16; Hebrews 13:5
loose morals	James 1:12; 2Timothy 2:15
looting	1 Samuel 23:1; Ephesians 4:28
loving evil	Psalm 52:3; Psalm 57:10
	Romans12:9
loving money	Matthew 6:24; 1 Timothy 6:10
loving praise	Philippians 2:3-4
lust	Matthew 5:28; Galatians 5:16
lust of the eye	Matthew 5:28; 1 John 2:16
	Psalm 119:37
lust of the flesh	1 John 2:16
lust of the mind	Psalm 25:11; Psalm 38:18

lying to the Holy Spirit	Acts 5:1-5; Proverb 12:22
lying with pleasure & delight	Colossians 3:9-10; Proverbs 12:19
madness	John 10:20; Jeremiah 50:38
magic	Acts 8:9-13; Ezekiel 13:18
making war	Micah 3:5; Psalm 140:2; Job 38:23
maliciousness	Exodus 23:1; Proverbs 17:4
manipulation	Galatians 2:4; 2 Corinthians 11:20
manslaughter	Matthew 5:21; Exodus 23:7
marauding	Joshua 8:27; 1 Samuel 15:19
masturbation	James 1:14-15; 1 Corinthians 10:13
materialism	Luke 12:15; Matthew 6:19-21
mischief	Ephesians 4:1-3; Proverbs 12:16
misery	Exodus 3:7; Judges 10:16
misleading	Matthew 18:6-7; 2 Chronicles 32:15
mulishness	Leviticus 26:19; Psalm 81:12
mocking	Proverbs 17:5; 2 Peter 3:3-7
murder	Exodus 20:13; Numbers 35:12
murmuring	Philippians 2:14; James 5:8
muttering	Isaiah 8:19; Lamentations 3:62
necromancy	Leviticus 19:31; 1 John 4:1
negativism	Matthew 7:1-2; 2 Corinthians 10:5 Romans 15:5-6
nicotine addiction	1 Corinthians 6:19-20; 3:17
not being watchful	Matthew 24:24; John 4:48
occultism	Isaiah 8:18; 2 King 21:6
obsessing	2 Corinthians 10:4-5; Philippians 4:8
obstinacy	1 John 3:2; Hebrews 4:12
oppression	Deuteronomy 26:7; Job 35:9
overbearing	Titus 1:7
pedophilia	Leviticus 18:23, 20:12; Mark 9:42
persecuting believers	2 Timothy 3:12; John 15:18
persecuting, persecution	Acts 9:11; John 15:18; 1 Peter 3:14 Matthew 5:10
perversion	Leviticus 18:23; Romans 1:27

perverting the gospel	Acts 20:20; Galatians 1:7
petulance	Isaiah 40:32; Job 38:4
planning without God	Proverbs 16:9; Matthew 6:34
plotting	Ezekiel 11:2; Proverbs 16:30
plundering	Ezekiel 39:10
pompousness	1 Timothy 4:13; 1 John 4:6
pornography	Psalm 101:3; Proverbs 6:25-27
possessiveness	Mark 12:27; Malachi 3:17 Ephesian 4:28
pouting	Proverbs 14:17, 15:18; James 1:19
prayerlessness	1 Thessalonians 5:17; John 15:7 Philippians 4:6
prejudice	Galatians 3:28; Titus 1:12-13 Ephesians 4:32
presumption	2 Peter 3:1-18; 1 Corinthians 2:14
pretending to be a prophet	2 Peter 2:1-22; 2 Timothy 3:16
pretension	2 Corinthians 10:5
pridefulness	Proverbs 11:2; Proverbs 29:23
pride of life	1 John 2:16; Proverbs 27:2 Jeremiah 9:23
procrastination	1 Peter 5:7; Psalm 39:7
profane God, His holiness	Colossians 3:8; Ephesians 4:29
profanity unto God	1 Timothy 6:10; Psalm 34:13
professing to be wise	James 1:1-27
prophecy by Baal	Deuteronomy 18:15; Matthew 24:11
prophesying lies	1 John 4:1
propagating lies	Exodus 5:9; Proverbs 19:5
proudness	James 4:6; Proverbs 16:5
provoking God	Deuteronomy 4:25; 1 Kings 16:7
provoking	Galatians 5:26; Jeremiah 7:19
puffing up	1 Samuel 17:28; Galatians 5:26 Colossian 2:18
quarreling	Genesis 13:8; 1 Corinthians 3
quenching the Holy Spirit	Solomon 8:7; Amos 5:6

questioning God's Word	Isaiah 55:8-9; 1 Corinthians 2:16
raiding	Proverbs 24:15
railing	Proverb 102.8
raging	Psalm 37:8; Romans 12:21
	Proverbs 15:1
raping	Deuteronomy 22:25-28; Psalm 82:3
rationalization	Luke 14:18-20; Genesis 3:13
ravaging	1 Chronicles 21:12; Acts 8:1-40
rebellion	Psalm 106.43; 1 Samuel 15:23
	Proverbs 17:11
rebuking	2 Timothy 3:16; Proverb 27:5
recklessness	Numbers 22:32; Judges 9:4
refusing to hear	Matthew 11:15; Exodus 19:9
refusing to repent	Jeremiah 15:19; 1 John 1:9
refusing to be humble	1 Chronicles 7:14; James 4:6
refusing to live in peace	Romans 5:1; Philippians 4:7
rejecting reproof, salvation	Proverbs 5:12, 6:23
rejecting God and His Word	Luke 9:23; Matthew 10:32
	Galatians 1:8-9
rejection	Romans 11:15; Hosea 4:6
	1 Peter 2:4
rejoicing in others' adversity	Colossians 2:18
rejoicing in idols	1 Corinthians 10:14
rejoicing in iniquity	John 14:1-31
repetitiveness	Hebrews 10:26
reproaching good men	Job 27:6; Proverbs 79:12
resentment	Judges 8:3; Job 5:2; Job 36:13
restlessness	Genesis 4:12; James 3:8
retaliation	Matthew 5:39; Matthew 6:15
reveling	1 Samuel 30:16; Isaiah 23:12
	2 Peter 2:13
reviling	Matthew 5:11, 15:4
revenge	Leviticus 19:18; Romans 12:19
rigidity	Mark 9:18; Matthew 11:28-39

robbing God	Malachi 3:8
robbery	Philippians 2:6; Isaiah 61:8
	Ezekiel 18:7
rudeness	Matthew 5:22; Proverbs 15:23
sadism	Nahum 3:19; Psalm 71:4
	Proverbs 11:17
scheming	Ester 9:25; Ezekiel 38:10
	Ecclesiastes 7:25, 27
scornfulness	1 Samuel 2:29; Psalm 64:8
	Galatians 4:14
seduction	Acts 18:13; Habakkuk 1:3
seeking self-gain	Matthew 6:33; Psalm 27:8
seek pleasures from world	Matthew 6:33; 1 Chronicles 22:19
self-accusations	1 Corinthians 3:16-17
self-admiration	1 Corinthians 3:16-17
self-centeredness	Matthew 16:24
self-condemnation	1 Peter 3:3-4; Matthew 16:24-25
	Romans 8:1-2
self-corruption	Luke 16:15; Romans 12:3
self-criticalness	Proverbs 12:18
self-deception	2 Peter 3:9; Acts 14:15
self-delusion	Titus 1:11-12; Romans 8:7-9
self-destruction	Matthew 7:13-14; Psalm 97:2-7
self-exultation	Isaiah 45:25; Isaiah 14:8
self-glorification	Psalm 34:3; Psalm 69:30
self-hatred	Ephesians 5:29; Proverbs 10:18
	Proverbs 10:12
self-importance	Galatians 2:6; Mark 12:29
self-rejection	Psalm 34:17-20; Romans 8:1, 12:10
selfishness	Philippians 2:4; Galatians 6:2
self-pity	1 Thessalonians 5:18; James 5:13
self-righteousness	Luke 18:9-14; Matthew 6:7
self-seeking	Romans 2:8; 1 Corinthians 13:4-5
serving other gods	Joshua 24:15

sewing discord	Proverbs 6:16-19; Exodus 20:16
sexual idolatry	Matthew 5:28 1 Thessalonians 4:2-8
sexual immorality	1 Thessalonians 4:2-8 1 Corinthians 6:18-20
sexual impurity	1 Thessalonians 4:3-5 Galatians 5:19-21
sexual perversion	Leviticus 18:23; 20:13; Jude 1:7
oral sex	1 Corinthians 7:3-4; Solomon 2:3
sodomy	Leviticus 20:13; Romans 1:26
shame	Isaiah 61:7; Psalm 34:4-5
silliness	Proverbs 8:5; Romans 16:24
sinful mirth	Job 20:5
skepticism	Matthew 21:21; James 1:6
slander	Leviticus 19:16; Psalm 54:5 Proverbs 10:18
slaying	Psalm 34:21; Genesis 37:26
slothfulness	Proverbs 6:6; 19:15; Colossians 3:17
snobbishness	Romans 12:16; Psalm 2:1-22
soothsaying	Leviticus 20:6 Acts 19:19
sorcery	Leviticus 19:31; 1 Chronicles 10:13
sowing seeds of hatred	James 4:11; Proverbs 6:14
speaking curses	Isaiah 8:10; Jeremiah 48:10
speaking incantations	Ezekiel 13:20; Revelation 21:8
speaking folly	Job 42:8; Psalm 38:5 Proverbs 12:23
speculation	Matthew 12:37; Proverbs 13:3
spell-casting	Matthew 10:28; 1 Corinthians 2:11
spiritual laziness	Proverbs 19:16; Proverbs 13:4
spitefulness	1 Peter 2:1-25; 1 Timothy 2:1-15
stealing	Ephesians 4:28; Proverbs 10:23
stiff-necked	Exodus 32:9; Deuteronomy 10:16
strife	Proverbs 20:3; Proverbs 17:1
striving over leadership	Colossians 3:23-24; Acts 20:28

struggling	1 Corinthians 10:13; Romans 8:18
stubbornness	Psalm 81:11-12; Romans 2:5
stupidity	Romans 1:22; Proverbs 12:1
	Proverbs 14:16-18
suicidal thoughts	James 4:7; 1 Corinthians 3:16-17
	Ecclesiastes 7:17
suspicion	Hebrews 11:6; Proverbs 3:5
swearing	James 5:12; Matthew 5:34-37
taking advantage of others	Luke 6:31; 1 Thessalonians 4:6
taking a bribe	Exodus 23:8; Deuteronomy 16:19
taking offense	1 Samuel 25:28; Job 10:14,13:23
taking God's Name in vain	Matthew 12:23
taking rights from poor	Ezekiel 18:16,18
teaching false doctrines	1 Timothy 1:3, 6:3
temper	1 Samuel 20:7; Proverbs 16:32
temptation	Matthew 6:13, 26:14
tempting God	James 1:13
theft	Matthew 15:19
timidity	2 Timothy 1:7
trickery, two-facedness	Genesis 3:1; Matthew 24:24
trustless	Numbers 20:12
trusting lies	Psalm 118:8; Galatians 6:3
trusting own righteousness	John 14:1; Jeremiah 48:7
trusting wickedness	John 12:36
tumults	Amos 2:2; Galatians 1:7, 5:10
turning your back on God	Matthew 10:33; Ephesians 6:11
unbelief	Mark 9:24; Romans 4:20
unbridled lust	1 Thessalonians 4:4
uncleanness	Matthew 12:43; Ezekiel 44:23
uncompromising	James 4:17; Galatians 5:16
undermining	Job 15:4
unequal yoked no-believers	2 Corinthians 6:14
unfairness	Matthew 20:13
unfaithfulness	Leviticus 6:2; Deuteronomy 32:20

un-forgiveness	Mark 11:25
unfriendliness	Proverbs 18:1
ungratefulness	Luke 6:35; 2 Timothy 3:2
unholy alliances	1 Kings 3:1; Isaiah 30:1
unholy habits	1 Timothy 5:13; Hebrews 10:25
unmanly	Genesis 1:26
un-mercifulness	Matthew 18:21; Jude 1:22
unrepentant	1 John 1:9; Revelation 2:5
unrighteousness	Jeremiah 22:13; Romans 3:5 1 John 1:9
unruliness of tongues	Micah 6:13; Psalm 120:2
usury	Nehemiah 5:10; 5:7; Psalm 15:5 Ezekiel 18:13
unthankful	Colossians 3:15, 4:2
untruthfulness	Proverbs 12:17, 14:5
Unworthiness	Luke 17:10; 1 Corinthians 11:27
using tarot cards	Leviticus 20:6; Mark 13:1-37
vain imaginations	Zachariah 10:2; Philippians 2:3
vanity	1 Samuel 16:7; Ecclesiastes 5:10
vengeance	Romans 12:19; Matthew 5:38-39
viciousness	Matthew 26:52-54; Psalm 11:5
violence	Job 16:17; Obadiah 1:10
vulgarity	Ephesians 4:29, 5:4 1 Thessalonians 5:22
white magic	Leviticus 19:31; 1 John 4:1
wickedness	1 Timothy 5:8; Ezekiel 33:11
willful sin	Hebrews 10:26; 1 John 3:4
willful and/or intentional sin	Numbers 3:1-51; Hebrews 10:26
winking with evil intent	Job 15:12; Proverbs 3:29
witchcraft, withdrawal	Deuteronomy 18:9-12, 18:20 Micah 5:12
withholding a pledge	Proverb 3:27, 23:13
without concern	1 Timothy 6:20; Acts 24:23
without natural affection	John 13:34-35; Ephesians 4:31-32

without mercy	Luke 6:36; Matthew 5:7
working for praise	Galatians 5:16-26; 1 John 2:16
	Galatians 6:7-9
worldliness	1 John 2:15-17; Romans 12:2
worrying	Matthew 6:25-34; 1 Peter 5:7
	Matthew 10:19
worshipping possessions	Revelation 9:20; 1 John 2:15-17
worshipping our works	Romans 1:25
worshipping the creation	Romans 1:25
worshipping of planets	John 4:23
wrathfulness	Psalm 37:8; Romans 12:19
wrong doing	Exodus 23:2; Isaiah 1:16
zealous to make others sinful	Romans 10:2
zealousness in outward show	Philippians 1:27

References

Bible Gateway. Biblegateway.com. July 2014.

Bible Hub. Biblehub.com. August 2014.

Biblestudytools.com. September 2014.

Children bible story book. Lavistachurchofchrist.com.

Christ Notes. Christnotes.org. December 2014.

"Confessing." Merriam-Webster Dictionary. http://www.merriam-webster.com. December 2014.

Gill. J. *Gill's Exposition of the Entire Bible*. www.ewordtoday.com/comments/gill. July 2014.

Good News Translation. biblegateway.org.

Henry, M. *Matthew Henry's Commentary* www.Christnotes.org.

High Calling Ministries. http://www.thehighcalling.org

Openbible.info

Tyndale. (2003). *Life Application Study Bible* (KJV).

"Wicked." Dictionary.com. January 2015.

Wiersbe, W. W. *Bible Commentary*. (1991).Thomas Nelson Publishers.

WorldNet (r) 1.7. http://dictionary.die.net/fear

Zondervan. (2003). *NIV Quest Study Bible, Revised*. Grand Rapids, Michigan 49530.

About the Author

Minister Rayford Jones Elliott is a minister of the gospel of Jesus Christ. He is a devout follower of Christ Jesus because he loves the Lord with his whole heart. As a minister, he teaches and preaches the Word with great fervency in an attempt to save the lost by bringing them into the knowledge of the truth. In his local church, where he has been a member for fifteen years, Minister Elliott serves as the president of the Men's Fellowship. He conducts weekly discussion groups, thereby demonstrating his dedication to the spiritual development of men. It is his desire to instill in them the same love and zeal for Christ Jesus that he possesses.

www.ingramcontent.com/pod-product-compliance
Lightning Source LLC
Chambersburg PA
CBHW070248100426
42743CB00011B/2185